MANAGING TIME

The Inmate's Guide To
Serving Time Productively

Vanessa —
You are destined to
do great exploits in the
area of law!

LALO GOMEZ

MANAGING TIME
The Inmate's Guide To Serving Time Productively
388 Bullsboro Drive #338
Newnan, GA 30263
Email: managingtime247@gmail.com

ISBN # 978-1-943343-23-2

Cover Design:
Eduardo Marroquin III, Front Cover
Moyses "Moy" Melgar, Back Cover

PublishAffordably.com / 773.783.2981

This book is dedicated
To the memory of my father
October 5, 1937 - March 31, 2008

Precious in the sight of the Lord
is the death of his saints
Psalm 116:15

.

TABLE OF CONTENTS

Acknowledgements.. *i*

Preface.. *v*

Foreword... *vii*

Introduction... *ix*

Chapter One:

SPIRIT TIME 1

    Faith...4

    Hope...6

    Love 14

    Prayer...19

    Fasting..27

    Bible Study..30

    Chapel Activities 35

    Thought Provokers...36

Chapter Two:

SOUL TIME...37

    Education...38

    Work Detail 43

Computer Literacy 46
Cultivate Your Skills, Talents, and Gifts 47
Library 48
Thought Provokers 51

Chapter Three:
BODY TIME 52
Health 52
Weight Training 54
Calisthenics, Cardio and Chiropractic 57
Sports and Leisure Time Activities 60
Dieting 62
Rest 67
Body Killers 69
Thought Provokers 71

Chapter Four:
MONEY TIME 72
Manage It 73
Tithe It 74
Give It 75
Save It 80
Budget It 83
Invest It 85
Spend It 86
Thought Provokers 87

Chapter Five:
SOCIAL TIME 88
Reconcile Strained Relationships 89

Build New Relationships 95
Make Amends to the Victim 101
Invest Time in Your Children 103
Train Yourself to Be an Effective
      Communicator and Listener............................110
Writing...117
Comprehension...122
People Skills 125
Community-Based Organizations 129
Volunteer 133
Self-Help Group..138
Thought Provokers..141

ADDENDUM

Conclusion..144
Reminders for Managing Time..............................150
Suggested Readings 152
Time Thieves / Time Tools 156
About the Author 157

MANAGING TIME: THE INMATE'S GUIDE TO SERVING TIME PRODUCTIVELY

Acknlowledgments

I give thanks and praise first and foremost to my Lord and Savior Jesus Christ, whom without the writing of this book would not have been possible. Thank You, Jesus, for bringing me out of darkness into Your wonderful light, and for teaching me how to manage time. You are the reason I was able to manage time productively during my incarceration, why I'm able to manage time productively post-incarceration, and why I can continue to share this priceless knowledge with others who desire to be faithful stewards of that one thing we cannot get back once it's gone: TIME! To You be the honor, the glory and the power, forever and ever! Amen.

Since God made it possible for my parents to bring me into this world, I am honored to acknowledge them next. Mom, mere words could never fully express how much I love you, how fortunate I am to have you in my life, and how grateful I am for the unconditional love and unwavering support you and Dad showed me during the quarter century I spent incarcerated. You and Dad were there for me when I needed you most, and even though Dad went home to be with the Lord, I commit myself to be there for you now that I am back in your fold. *Bendición!*

To my wife: *you are the love of my life.* You were there for me during the most difficult years I spent incarcerated. You lifted me up when I

i

was down, made me smile when I wasn't feeling it, and helped me stay sane in an otherwise insane environment. There aren't enough words for me to express how I feel about you and how blessed I am to have you in my life. Suffice it to say I loved you then, I love you now, and I'll love you forever. Partners For Life!

To my children, and grandchildren, *I am blessed to be back in your fold.* I'm proud of your achievements and the individuals you've become. I know that God is truly working in and through you for His glory. Thank you for making me a young granddad (lol). You rock! Let's keep it moving and never look back. Much love!

To my brothers and sister and all the rest of my family: Each one of you helped to make my incarceration more bearable just by being there for me. Words alone cannot express my gratitude. Love you much. *Family for life!*

To my long-time friend and writing mentor, Jeff Evans: God allowed our paths to cross at a time when I needed an accomplished writer to help me take my God-given gift of writing to the next level. *I will always be grateful for the years you invested in me.* Shalom!

A very special shout out goes out to Senior Pastors, Jerry and Chris McQuay (CLC.TV's awesome spiritual parents), and to all of my CLC.TV family, especially those CLCers who have served faithfully throughout the years, and all those who have "stepped up" at each campus. When God needs a "Few Good Saints," *you are on point.* Your reward is exceedingly great! May the Lord bless each of you abundantly as you advance the kingdom by Loving God, Serving Others, Reaching Nations.

Kudos to Pastor Ed Marroquin, III: *You are a media guru and genuine friend.* Thanks for all the work you did with the front cover. It looks awesome. Stay blessed!

To Moyses "Moy" Melgar: Thank you for hooking up the back cover, you are truly a servant-leader with a phenomenal skill set.

To Jon Jones and the awesome AOH team: *You were supernaturally "Created, Called and Uniquely Gifted to Reproduce the Atmosphere of Heaven on Earth!"* Thank you for allowing Almighty God to use you to be a carrier and producer of His sound, that powerful gift of worship that He purposed to get into the Earth realm through His Body. Y'all rock!

To CLC's Servants of Praise: *You are—in my humble opinion—the best praise and worship saints in all of Chicagoland!* What you do each time you get on stage prepares hearts to believe and receive the Word of God, and is near and dear to the Father's heart. May our good, good, Father bless each of you abundantly for leading CLCers into His presence in such a Spirit-filled, anointed, and powerful way, week after week!

To my brother and friend, Carl Banks: *You are one of the most dedicated servant-leaders I know.* Thank you for the opportunity to serve alongside you on the Facilities Team. It was a blessing to be part of this vital ministry. Love you maaaan!

To Joshua Morris, my Bible teacher and mentor-in-Christ: *I love you brother for helping me grow in the Word. I will never be the same!*

To George W. Knox, Ph.D., *America's leading expert on all things gang-related!* Thank you so much for planting that seed in me all those years ago to write. You believed in me and encouraged me at a time when I needed to be reminded that despite my circumstances, I still had the ability to rise above all that and to excel. That positive reinforcement enabled me to manage the remainder of my sentence as productively as I did. You then blessed me with the opportunity to shine by allowing me to enlightening others at the NGCRC Conference once I was released. That was an experience I'll never forget. I thank God for using you to coach me on how to be a "better me" instead of the me I used to be. Know that your earthly and eternal rewards are exceeding abundantly above all you can ask or imagine. May the Lord bless you always!

To Ellis C. McCarthy: Thank you for following the Spirit's lead by introducing me to Marilyn when you did. Her level of expertise in this business has been invaluable to me and this book. You are truly the Blueprint of a God-Man!

To Marilyn Alexander: You are truly an anointed and talented publisher. Thank you for accepting my book project and making it a reality. Your wisdom, knowledge and depth of understanding of this business has helped to inspire me and countless others to use their God-given gift of writing to bless others in a big way. Thank you so much for being patient with me throughout the entire process, even when I seemed to be ducking and dodging you, lol. You once told me there is a season in which a book has to be written, published, and put in the hands of readers in order for its purpose to be fulfilled. I believe this is that season. America and the rest of the world's prison population will never be the same again! May the Lord continue to bless you and Joey (your multi-talented husband, wat up bro!), and your immensely-gifted kids, for being faithful servant-leaders. Selah!

To everyone I didn't mention by name (*you're as numerous as the stars in the sky, lol*), you know who you are. May each of you be blessed in some way for blessing me in some way. Shalom!

Finally, to all of my brothers in Christ whom I had the privilege of "managing time" with, and to all incarcerated men and women worldwide: *Time is what YOU make of it. Don't just serve it, manage it!*

PREFACE

This is a how-to guide regarding the application of time management in a correctional setting. The purpose of this book is to encourage and equip incarcerated men and women to serve their time productively, so that they will be prepared to make the challenging transition back to society and avoid reoffending. This is a win-win for all of society because it lowers recidivism.

For those who are long term residents of the penal system, particularly those that do not have a release date, this how-to guide will encourage them to "redeem the time", that they might strive each day to be as productive as they can be and not allow their circumstances to limit their God-given potential.

It is the author's firm belief that the staggering rate of recidivism in the United States and abroad can be reduced significantly. It is time to stop *talking* about how to get this done, and start *acting* on the knowledge and resources we have to actually get it done. This book offers a proactive solution for how to get it done in real time, here and now, for anyone willing to apply its time-oriented principles. The author cites his successful transition from prison to society as evidence of this.

Shalom!

FOREWORD

I am sitting here, after reading this book, with tears in my eyes as I reflect on the words of a man who could have given up on life, but instead chose to allow God to change his heart and use "serving time" to serve Him. Lalo brings a new understanding to managing time, and he does it distinctly by breaking down priorities in life: Spirit Time, Soul Time, Body Time, Money Time, and Social Time. The message is a timely one, and it isn't just words on a page for the incarcerated, but practical insight into how each of us can honor God through managing time wisely.

I have been a pastor for over twenty years and have read many books on time management-related subjects, but this one is unique. The words that penetrated my heart through these pages will hopefully penetrate yours as well and move you to evaluate what you are doing with your time. As Lalo states in the very beginning, yesterday is history and tomorrow is a mystery, but each of us have today. If we took on the heart of this message and lived each moment in a way that is pleasing to God, I believe we would have less regrets, less heartache, more successes in life and relationships, and a lot less men and women reoffending and returning to jail or prison after being released.

This book will give those that read it an opportunity to evaluate their lives and their actions, and to really make life count by managing time wisely and fulfilling the purpose for which God created them. I challenge you to read this book with an open mind and a humble heart, completely willing to be examined by the Holy Spirit, and watch as this modern day disciple of Jesus Christ speaks words of life into your soul.

Thank you, Lalo, for allowing God to use you as a precise and powerful tool with this book to encourage and equip incarcerated men and women across the United States and the rest of the world to serve their time productively. This way they can make a successful transition in society and avoid contributing to the recidivism rate, by not reoffending, after they are released. I believe every incarcerated person that reads this book with an open mind and a humble heart will be encouraged and equipped to do just that.

Blessings,

Ben Stewart, Executive Pastor
CLC.TV

INTRODUCTION

For those of you who are incarcerated and are blessed to be reading this book, if you're wondering why I use the term "inmate" instead of "convict" in my subtitle and throughout this book, the answer is simple: I chose not to invest time sweating the small stuff, like focusing on whether to use inmate or convict. I chose instead to focus on content. That is what I encourage you to do as you read this book.

I began writing this book in the summer of 2005. I had been denied my third bid for clemency a few months earlier by a former Illinois governor who is now serving time in federal prison. My second bid for clemency had also been denied by a former Illinois governor; he too was in federal prison as of this writing, but has since been released. I find it ironic that they denied me a chance at freedom, and by their own doing wound up losing their own freedom. But having been through twenty-four years of incarceration, I would not wish prison on them or anyone else. My advice to those reading this book who have never been on the wrong side of the law: DON'T GO THERE!

I had two and a half years left to serve when I was denied clemency again. I was at a medium security facility where I had spent the past fifteen years and wanted to transfer to a minimum security facility to serve the remainder of my sentence. So, I submitted a transfer request and waited to see if it would be approved. About a month later I received word from my counselor that my transfer request had been approved and that I would be transferred the following day. The Illinois Department of Corrections (IDOC) allows inmates to choose one of three facilities to transfer to, but the Department itself makes the final decision which facility an inmate will be transferred to. Such was the case with me. I was hoping, praying and believing to be transferred to the best minimum security prison in Illinois, but I ended up at one of the worst instead. The housing unit set-up was dorm style; twenty inmates to a room.

The minute I walked into the housing unit I was assigned to I knew I would not be able to serve the remainder of my sentence at this prison, even though I had just two and a half years left. The reason being, I went from a two-man cell at the facility I had just been transferred from, to a twenty-man cell at the facility I had just been transferred to. It was then that I realized I had made a mistake requesting to be transferred. My mistake was not getting with God first in prayer to seek His will in the matter.

I repented and asked God for forgiveness, and to make it possible for me to be transferred back to the facility I was transferred from. God answered that prayer quickly. I was transferred the following day! I had favor with an IDOC higher-up whom I had known since he was an officer, and God made it possible for this individual to bypass all the red tape involved with a transfer. And no, I wasn't his "snitch"! I serve an awesome God who is able to do exceeding abundantly above all we could ever ask or imagine (Ephesians 3:20).

A few days later, while walking the yard alone, I began thinking what I would do with the two- and-a-half years I had left to serve. In my mind I had already done everything I could do at this facility to advance myself with the limited resources I had available, which is why I requested the transfer. But God already had my next project lined up. He impressed it upon me to write a book about something I had experience doing. The first thing that came to mind was "serving time," crazy as that might sound. I could have written about a lot of other things I had experienced, but serving time was the first thing that came to mind, so I listened to that still small voice and went with it.

I was excited about this new project because God gave me the vision, the purpose, the goal, and the objective. He let me know, in no uncertain terms, that this book will be used to encourage and equip incarcerated people to serve their time productively. In doing so, they will be prepared *spiritually, emotionally, physically, financially, and socially* to re-enter society upon their release. This will help them to make a successful transition and avoid reoffending. It will also help to break the cycle of recidivism in America and eventually the entire world. I serve an awesome God!

I finished the first draft of this book in eight months, but decided to wait until I was released to revise it simply because I had no desire to use a typewriter again. The book you are holding in your hands is the finished product. It is the culmination of smart work, discipline, and consistency; three important things I learned and subsequently applied during the years I spent serving time productively. The time I invested writing this book during my incarceration, and then revising it after I was released was a valuable investment of time. It is an investment that will continue to yield me profitable returns for many years to come; not just financially, but spiritually, emotionally, physically, and socially as well.

I believe we are living on allotted time and that managing time is more significant today than it has ever been. It does not matter whether you are incarcerated or not, or whether you are a believer or an unbeliever. This is a reality that pertains to every living soul on this planet, one that no man, woman, or child is exempt from.

Having spent twenty-four years of my life incarcerated (sixteen of which I served productively) I believe I've earned the right to write about the important and oftentimes neglected issue of serving time, which I also refer to as "managing time." I am not writing about this issue because I know more about managing time than anyone else who has served time, but because I learned how to master the application of time management in a correctional setting by committing myself to doing it. Now I am able to reapply these principles in society on a daily basis, where one must guard his time zealously. Today I am reaping a harvest of "the seed I sowed on good ground" (the time I invested preparing myself to make the challenging transition back to society) over that sixteen-year period of productive incarceration.

One day each of us will stand before God to give an account for how we managed time. Therefore, I am totally committed to managing time each and every day as productively as possible. When that day comes for me to give an account, I want to be able to stand before God and hear Him say "Well done, good and faithful servant!" (Matthew 25:21).

If you are incarcerated and are serious about serving time productively, so that when you are released you will have a better chance at making a successful transition and becoming a productive member of society, then you have your nose in the right book. The principles I share throughout this book are simple and practical and are meant to encourage and equip you to manage time in the near-term (during your incarceration), so that you will have a head start on managing time in the long term (when you are released).

One of the things I discovered throughout my incarceration is that inmates who serve time productively have a better chance of making a successful transition in society when they are released and are less likely to reoffend. Inmates who neglect to serve time productively contribute to the recidivism rate in large measure by returning to prison on a parole violation or another offense. If you are incarcerated, you alone must decide whether you are going to serve time productively or destructively. If you choose to be productive, you will apply what you learn in this book to prepare yourself to make a successful transition in society. If you choose to be destructive, you may be setting yourself up for another prison term. I am living proof that serving time productively works if you apply yourself. Repeat offenders prove that serving time destructively doesn't!

I saw both sides of that coin many times during my twenty-four years of incarceration, and throughout the years since my release from prison. The majority of those who served time productively and were released made a successful transition in society, whereas those who served time destructively and were released returned to prison on a parole violation or another offense; most of them on more than one occasion and most within thirty days of their release. I am determined to change this revolving cycle that has our jails and prisons full to capacity, and the damaging impact it has on society-at-large.

Managing time is not something that comes naturally to anyone, nor is it easily mastered by anyone. In a correctional setting, the bar is set even higher. An inmate has to have the desire, the discipline, and the determination to manage time on a consistent basis. It took several years for me to acquire the desire, the discipline and the determination to manage time consistently in each of the areas I cover in this book. I assure you, it was not an easy process. I went through a lot of trial and error until I finally got it right. My determination to manage time by serving it productively paid off, and yours will too. All you have to do is apply yourself.

Prison can be a difficult place to learn time management if you are not committed to it. I had to extricate myself from all of the negativity that goes on in the correctional setting in order to focus on managing time. Only then was I able to move forward and serve productively the time I was sentenced to.

The controlled and unpredictable nature of the correctional setting oftentimes presents obstacles that can stand in the way of an inmate becoming a successful time manager, with NEGATIVE THINKING being the leading obstacle. The Bible tells us *as a man thinks, so is he* (Proverbs 23:7). Gang activity and drug abuse, brought on by negative thinking, are the most destructive self-imposed obstacles that will keep you from managing time effectively during and after a period of incarceration simply because they will keep you focused on negativity.

If you are serving time and desire to be a disciplined and consistent time manager when you are released, you are going to have to discipline yourself to manage time consistently during your incarceration. Time is on your side while you are incarcerated, because you have time to train and discipline yourself to manage time. Do not think that you can wait until you are released to learn time management. You are in for a possible setback, because you will have more challenges to face in society than you did during your incarceration.

Why procrastinate and put off for tomorrow what you can start today? Think about it. Yesterday is history. Tomorrow is not promised to anyone. Today is all you have. Why not make the most of it by learning how to manage time so that you can overcome those obstacles now, while you are incarcerated? I know what it's like to mismanage time, because I did it for the first eight years of my incarceration by needlessly getting myself caught up in all kinds of prison drama. I forfeited my freedom in 1984. It wasn't until 1992, that I came to the realization that I had wasted the previous eight-years of my life in prison doing nothing but digging a deeper hole for myself. One thing was certain, if I did not flip the script and start managing time instead of letting it manage me, I was sure to prolong my stay in prison way past my outdate.

As a matter of fact, I could have easily added life to my forty-eight year sentence (without the possibility of parole) or the death penalty, which meant I would have never been released, or I would have died an early death by lethal injection. Those were the harsh realities I was faced with, any of which could have easily happened had I stayed on that reckless path; but God is merciful. He had different plans for me (Jeremiah 29:11).

When I woke up on that cold morning of January 1, 1992, after spending half the night praying, I knew then that I could not continue serving time as I had been doing. I still had sixteen years left to serve on my forty-eight year sentence (you get day-for-day in Illinois, which means you serve only half of your sentence, unless you are sentenced to serve eighty-five or one-hundred percent of your sentence), and if I was going to get my head out of the sand and do something productive with my time, it had to begin then and there. That was my wake-up call, and it came at the perfect time. God's timing is always perfect. It was time to train and discipline myself to manage time.

While praying that night I asked God to forgive me for all the years I had spent living recklessly on the streets, running wild since the age of twelve, as well as the first eight years of my incarceration. I gave thanks to God, that because of His love, mercy, and grace I was still alive. It was then that I asked Him to teach me how to apply wisdom in the area of time management so that I could train and discipline myself to manage wisely the time I had left to serve.

Once I awoke to the realization that I had forfeited so much time, I knew I could not afford to forfeit another moment. I knew I had to get focused with the business of managing the remainder of my sentence as productively as I could in order to prepare myself to make a successful transition in society when I was released. I was not only determined to manage the remainder of my sentence productively, but once God taught me how to do it effectively, I set out to teach other inmates who were serious about managing time to do the same. I, too, wanted them to be prepared to make a successful transition in society upon their release. Giving is a part of my DNA. I wanted to give to others what God so graciously gave to me.

If you are going to be an example to others, you have to lead by example; that is exactly what I did. I stopped chasing after things that did not matter and invested time in the things that did. How else would I be able to honor God and give Him the glory for teaching me how to become an effective time manager? He blessed me with wisdom in managing time so that I could apply it in my life and be able to share it with others during and after my incarceration. The book you are holding in your hands is the fruit of that labor.

There is an art and science to everything you do in life. Mastering the art and science of time management did not happen for me overnight. It took several years to get it right. I experienced as many setbacks as I did successes. But in the final analysis, it was worth the time and effort I put into it. Managing time while incarcerated (once I began doing it) is the catalyst that enabled me to write this book.

A person can do anything he or she sets their mind to. I set my mind to writing this book and did it. Never allow anyone to tell you that you cannot accomplish something. If you have a desire to do something positive, then do it. Sow seed on good soil and expect a harvest (Matthew 13:23). When you pray, believe that you receive it by faith and it will be yours (Mark 11:24). It will come to you at the appointed time.

Managing time God's way is the catalyst that has enabled me to make a successful transition in society and has kept me from desiring a return to my former way of life. I am not one to look back. If you know the story of Lot and what happened to his wife, after being warned not to look back at what was happening to Sodom, then you know that looking back to take even a glance at anything negative you might desire to go back to is the equivalent of playing Russian Roulette with your life. I am not going out like that and neither should you. At the end of the day that is a choice that you alone can make. I pray that you will make the right choice, one that will make it possible for you to be released from prison when you are supposed to be and keep you from reoffending.

My purpose, which I am passionate about, is to encourage and equip as many incarcerated men and women as possible to serve their time productively, so that when they are released they will be prepared to make the challenging transition back to society and avoid reoffending. This will reduce the recidivism rate significantly, which is one of the primary goals of this book.

Managing time benefitted me immensely during my incarceration in each of the five areas I cover in this book. Now it is benefitting me in society in these same key areas of life. Let serving time productively benefit you during your incarceration, so that you can benefit from it when you are released. You will see such a change in your entire approach to life that you will desire to do nothing with your time, but manage it productively.

> *"Be very careful, then, how you live—not as unwise but as wise, making the most of every opportunity, because the days are evil" Ephesians 5:15-16*

All scripture quotations are taken
from the Holy Bible
New International Version (NIV)

One

SPIRIT TIME

"There is a time for everything, and a season for every activity under heaven." - **Ecclesiastes 3:1**

I believe that everything in life revolves around the spiritual, and that God has everything under His sovereign control. Since I believe this, it was fitting that I write about this area of time management first.

I accepted Jesus Christ as my Savior and Lord the day after I was arrested. Although I believe my conversion was genuine I soon backslid to my gang banging ways, because I allowed myself to believe that I could be a Christian and a gang member at the same time. The devil's a liar!

Being incarcerated did not deter me from engaging in criminal activity. If anything, it enabled me to become a more hardened and sophisticated criminal. After spending five years in prison, during which time I slowly but surely began to realize that my life was headed nowhere really fast, I decided to walk away from gang life. I simply did not want to live that life anymore after having lived it religiously, 24-7, for fifteen years; that could only be the work of the Holy Spirit. God had a purpose for my life and it did not include spending the rest of it incarcerated or dying an early death while incarcerated, either of which could have easily happened.

When I rededicated my life to Jesus Christ in January of 1992, things began to change for the better. I had already mismanaged the first eight years of my forty-eight year sentence and was determined not to mismanage another moment. I enrolled in college classes, studied diligently daily, and within three years I received an Associate's degree. It took three years to earn that degree only because the IDOC stopped offering college classes from 1993-1995 at the facility I was housed at. Their reason: NOT ENOUGH INMATES SIGNED UP PER SEMESTER TO JUSTIFY OFFERING CLASSES.

However, when God opens a door, no one can close it (Revelation 3:8). By the grace of God I earned my Associates degree in May of 1997. I learned many other skills, as well, and became a model inmate in the eyes of prison officials who, after years of butting heads with me, decided to give me a chance to prove that even the worst of the worst can change for the better. I did exactly that once I began to serve time productively.

Engaging in spiritually-related activities while incarcerated is a productive way to manage time. If you do it while you are incarcerated, you will find yourself more inclined to do it after you are released. Doing this has helped me to stay focused on the things that matter most (i.e. God, family, others, health, business). Had I not applied time management in this area of my life while I was incarcerated, I probably would not be applying it in my life today.

Before I proceed, let me just say that I am not promoting man's *finite* wisdom in this chapter or in any chapter of this book. I rely solely on the *infinite* wisdom of God. He alone is in the driver's seat of my life. Therefore, before I put my hand to any project or make any decision, big or small, I consult with God first through prayer and by seeking guidance and direction from His life instruction manual, *the Bible.*
What I *am* promoting is the application of time management in a correctional setting, be it a county jail, or a state or federal correctional facility. The principles I share throughout this book are simple,

practical and universal in nature, meaning they can be applied by any incarcerated person regardless of his or her religious beliefs. I have made points of reference throughout this book from a Biblical perspective, because I believe in God and chose to use the Bible as my authoritative guide.

For those of you who do not believe in God, you can breathe easy. My purpose in this book is not to criticize, judge, or preach to you, but instead, to encourage and equip you on the importance of managing time. In doing so, you will hopefully serve your time productively (if you are not already doing so), and be able to make a successful transition in society when you are released.

Because I believe in God, I would be dishonoring Him and doing a disservice to fellow believers if I did not share in this book what I believe are sound Biblical principles regarding the areas I cover. How you choose to apply these principles, be it from a spiritual perspective or a worldly perspective, is between you and God. I am simply planting a seed in the lives of those who read this book, and believe they can benefit from it. Someone else may come along and water that seed, but only God can cause it to grow (1 Corinthians 3:7).

As I stated in the introduction of this book, managing time is not something I mastered overnight. Once I rededicated my life to God and became spiritually grounded, I began to train myself to manage my time effectively. I chose to apply the wisdom God gives us in the Bible to achieve the desired result, and in the process I became an effective time manager. Man's wisdom is finite. God's wisdom is infinite!

I believe I was able to become an effective time manager, because I invested time applying spiritually related attributes and involving myself in spiritually related activities, while training myself to manage soul time, body time, money time, and social time. You might choose to train yourself to manage time effectively by applying it in one of the other areas of this book first. I chose spirit time first. This enabled me to become effective at managing time in the other four areas (soul time, body time, money time, and social time).

> *"...managing time is not something I mastered overnight."*

At the end of each day (lock-up time), I felt good about myself because it was another day that I had served time productively, which in prison was a very good feeling. You too can feel good about yourself each and every day of your incarceration, if you commit yourself to serving your time productively. One of the ways that you can do this is by applying the following spiritually related attributes, and getting involved in the following spiritually related activities.

FAITH

This is the first and most important attribute you need to develop if you desire to manage time effectively from a spiritual standpoint. Without faith, you might find it hard to move forward, because faith is the key that unlocks our true potential. You will need faith to develop the desire to manage time regarding the important topics I will cover in this chapter and throughout this book.

So what is faith? In a nutshell, *faith is being sure of what we hope for and certain of what we do not see* (Hebrews 11:1). Our Creator (God) desires for us to possess faith, a source of unlimited, unshakable power that only He can provide us with. Man cannot give it. In today's society, practically everything is opposed to it simply because faith is something that no human being can see, hear, smell, taste, or touch. If it isn't material, most people don't want anything to do with it. We live in a materialistic society.

To operate in the realm of faith and make it work for you, it is imperative that you accept God's Word as truth, even in the midst of contradictory circumstances, when the world around you is saying it cannot be done. Faith is the only language God understands, for by it He spoke the universe into existence out of nothing (Hebrews 11:3). He declared that it was to be and it was (Genesis 1:3). We too, can operate in this realm, but we must believe it to receive it (Mark 11:24). We must invest time practicing these principles. (James 1:22).

The problem with most of us is that we think and speak negatively, and then wonder why things do not happen as they should. The Bible tells us in Proverbs 23:7 *as a man thinks so is he.* In like manner, when we speak negatively we have sowed negativity, and will reap negativity (Galatians 6:8). By our words we will be acquitted and by our words we will be condemned (Matthew 12:37). Negative thinking and negative speaking almost always leads to negative actions. If you think and speak positively, the result will always be positive. That isn't just common sense, that's God-sense.

So how do you develop faith? It takes a simple act of your will. Anyone can have faith, even if it is as small as a mustard seed (Matthew 13:31-32). We cannot work for it. We must work toward it. Faith without works is dead (James 2:26). That means we have to put in the work (i.e., invest time getting to know God through His Word, and by communicating with Him through prayer). We develop faith by maintaining a close relationship with our Creator. The power of faith lies in our ability to believe in that which we cannot attain through our natural senses.

> *"We partner with God and He gives us the ability to do everything His Word says we can do."*

When we invest time cultivating this powerful attribute, we develop the ability to *call the things that be not as though they were* (Romans 4:17). When we are ready to invest time on faith, God is ready to move in there with us to let the strength, power and force of faith manifest itself. We do not do it alone. We partner with God and He gives us the ability to do everything His Word says we can do. Apart from Him we can do nothing (John 15:5). But through Him we can do **ALL** things because He strengthens us (Philippians 4:13).

What better way is there to manage time than to invest time developing and exercising this powerful gift called faith? During my incarceration I used to invest time every morning, before my feet even touched the ground, praising and giving thanks to God for granting me a peaceful night's sleep and for blessing me with another day of life. It takes a simple act of faith to do that. I would then commit the day to Him, believing by faith that He would enable me in His strength, peace, patience, and wisdom to endure another day of incarceration. I found it to be a productive way to begin each day, which in turn enabled me to manage time effectively each day. I still do this each morning, and then praise and thank Him throughout the day, and again before I go to bed, for *it is good to proclaim His love in the morning and His faithfulness at night* (Psalm 92:1-2). You, too, can manage time each day by investing time developing, cultivating, and exercising faith. Take that bold leap of faith today. God has your back!

HOPE

How do you define hope? Webster's dictionary defines hope as being "something you desire with confident expectation of it being fulfilled." The Bible defines hope as *"something that does not disappoint us"* (Romans 5:5). Without hope, life in a correctional setting, or in any setting, can become difficult, boring, monotonous, and eventually meaningless. But with hope you can approach each new day with confidence that God is with you and watching over your every step. Our Creator knows the plans He has for you; *plans to give you **hope** and **a future*** (Jeremiah 29:11).

It's easy to lose hope in a correctional setting for any number of reasons (i.e. broken relationships with family, relatives, or friends; loss of a loved one; having to serve a sentence of life without parole and/ or one of many years of incarceration; an appeal and/or request for clemency (early release) denied, etc.) I encourage you, therefore, to invest time daily keeping this vital attribute alive. If you want to survive, keep hope alive!

If you ever get to the point where hope seems lost and despair sets in, do what I used to do: Remind yourself that God is still in control, that He will never leave you nor forsake you (Deuteronomy 31:8). If you're thinking it's easy for me to say that because I'm no longer incarcerated, trust me, it isn't. As I mentioned in the introduction, there are more obstacles standing in your way in society than there are in prison.

I've experienced this in many ways since my release, particularly where it concerns employment rejections because of my criminal background. But thanks be to God that *"In all these things we are more than conquerors through him who loved us"* (Romans 8:37). Be encouraged and know that *"...in all things God works for the good of those who love him, who have been called according to his purpose"* (Romans 8:28).

While I was incarcerated I invested time placing my hope in the One who created me, and since I have been out, that same hope has not disappointed me (Romans 5:5). God is the Author of hope, and when He is in the driver's seat of our lives, there is always hope; not only for today, but for tomorrow as well.

Everyone is entitled to their own opinion about whatever it is they choose to have an opinion about. I have my own opinion about life, one that derives from my belief that God is our Creator and is, therefore, in control of everything that exists, including every detail of our lives. Again, that is *my* opinion and I'm expressing it in this book from a Christian's perspective regarding time management and how to apply it in each of the areas covered herein. You are free to agree or disagree with my opinions and beliefs. I am expressing them because I believe there are more inmates who will agree with what is written in this book than those who will not. Remember, the primary purpose of this book is to educate those who read it about the importance of managing time in a correctional setting, and to encourage and equip them to do so. If only one inmate benefits from this book by applying its principles during his/her incarceration, then it has served its primary purpose. I believe wholeheartedly that more than one inmate will benefit from this book.

> *"I am of the opinion and belief that the inmate who does not believe God exists may find it difficult to have hope if he is facing years of incarceration..."*

I am of the opinion and belief that the inmate who does not believe God exists may find it difficult to have hope if he is facing years of incarceration, and/or serving a life sentence without parole. It does not matter how "hard" (tough) an inmate might think he is. I speak from experience because I carried myself that way when I first began serving my forty-eight year sentence. I used to act hard, but that was a facade that I put on to mask the hurt I was feeling inside at being away from my family.

Managing time cultivating this attribute we call "hope" was anything but easy. The thought of having to serve half of my forty-eight year sentence (twenty-four years) if I did not win one of my appeals and get a new trial (at which time I could plead guilty in exchange for a lesser sentence), was nothing short of overwhelming. And when I began to lose my appeals, my chance of getting a sentence reduction went out the window. My hope for a brighter day almost did as well!

Every inmate has his highs and lows (good days and bad days). I had my share of both during my incarceration. At one point I became so stressed about the length of time I had yet to serve (twelve years to be exact) that I almost committed suicide. That is how hopeless my situation felt at the time. It happened one Friday evening after I was taken to segregation (seg, aka, disciplinary confinement) for threatening an inmate. To give you a gist of what happened, I got into a verbal confrontation with this inmate after he made some comments about me to a Captain. He felt so threatened by me that he went back and told the Captain I threatened him with bodily harm, which I didn't, and the Captain had me placed in seg for threats and intimidation, a disciplinary infraction that carries six months across the board (six months seg, six months loss of good time, six months loss of privileges, etc.).

When I walked into that filthy seg cell with no running water, no lights, no mattress, and a sink and toilet that were so nasty I wouldn't even allow my dog to use it, all I could do was shake my head in frustration. As I paced the cell that night all types of thoughts ran through my mind, particularly the thought of kicking myself in the rear for putting myself in that predicament after making such good forward progress during the previous five years. Engaging in that verbal confrontation with this inmate was out of character for me, because I did not carry myself that way anymore. But I allowed my former way of thinking and reacting to situations to get the best of me that day and I paid for it.

It got so bad in that cell that I decided to take the easy way out. I was tired of serving time. I did not want to serve another twelve years. Just as the thought of ending my life ran through my mind, an officer came to the cell door and asked if I wanted to use the phone, even though seg inmates were not allowed to take a shower, use the phone, go to the yard, or even get the property they are allowed in seg until after spending twenty-four hours in seg. But God is good. I believe He sent that officer to my seg cell with the phone because He knew I was about to do something foolish and that was His way of keeping me from going there. Suffice it to say, it worked! I am alive and well today because of my Heavenly Father.

I called my mother because she is the first person who came to mind. I talked to her for about an hour, but did not tell her what I had almost done because that would have hurt her a lot. She consoled me as only a mother can, and I felt a lot better afterwards. I went to seg on Friday and was out the following Monday. God is good! I pled guilty to the disciplinary infraction and received only three days seg (time served), and thirty days C-grade (loss of privileges). I repented and got my heart right with God, because *He* is my hope through His Son Jesus Christ, and because I knew that without Him, hope would be elusive. God revealed to me time and time again through His Word that no matter how dismal one's situation might seem, we can have joy, peace, and "hope" simply by placing our trust in Him (Lamentations 3:21-26). That is how I survived twenty-four years of incarceration. If I had tried to go it alone, I would have crumbled under the weight of having to serve all of that time.

However, I did not crumble despite having to serve such a lengthy sentence. I mismanaged the first eight years of that sentence, but I managed the remaining sixteen productively and came out of it with a new lease on life. I chose to trust in the Lord with all my heart and lean not on my own understanding (Proverbs 3:5). I was able to manage time by keeping hope alive, and hope did not disappoint me, because God poured out His love into my heart by the Holy Spirit whom He had given me (Romans 5:5). He was all the hope I needed then, and He is all the hope I will ever need in this life. I will not trade that kind of assurance for anyone or anything.

> *"I can only encourage you to have faith in God through His Son Jesus Christ and receive the hope that is available to you through Him..."*

To those of you who do not believe that God exists, I encourage you to explore this further. If you do not believe anyone can prove to you that God exists, ask yourself this question: Can you prove to anyone that He doesn't? If you can't, then examine the Scriptures for yourself and let God reveal to you that His Word is true. That is what the Berean Christians did; they examined the Scriptures every day to see if what Paul said was true (Acts 17:11). *"Let God be true and every man a liar"* (Romans 3:4).

I can only encourage you to have faith in God through His Son Jesus Christ and receive the hope that is available to you through Him, but it is up to you to believe it and receive it (Mark 11:24). The hope that God can provide when you place your trust in Him will enable you to maintain a positive attitude, and help you manage time effectively each day of your incarceration no matter how dismal your situation might seem. *"We have this hope as an anchor for the soul, firm and secure"* (Hebrews 6:19).

There is a sharp contrast between the inmate who believes in Christ (the believer) and places his trust in Him, and the inmate who does not (the unbeliever). The believer has hope for today, tomorrow, and the future, regardless of his circumstances. The unbeliever does not by virtue of his unbelief.

The believer can manage time while incarcerated, whether he is soon to be released or not, because he has something real to hope for. In contrast, the inmate who does not believe in Christ and has not accepted His free gift of salvation, whether he is soon to be released or not, does not have anything real to hope for, and hence, has no real concept of time management. That is what I define as *being lost and wandering aimlessly through time.* Why? Because I have been there and done that in a way I never want to again. Life is too short and much too precious to spend even one day of it in that mindset, especially if you are incarcerated. God wants you to prosper so that you can have hope and a future (Jeremiah 29:11). Being incarcerated does not negate that; rejecting God does.

The believer has made the most important decision he will ever make by making Jesus Christ his hope. That inmate does not need a sign to believe that God is real. He will not spend time unproductively while incarcerated *"fixing his eyes on what is seen, for what is seen is temporary,*

11

but what is unseen is eternal" (2 Corinthians 4:18). Christ has made it possible for the believer to manage time while incarcerated no matter how dismal his situation might seem simply because He has given the believer the hope and promise of salvation and eternal life.

The believer who is fortunate enough to be released from prison will have a head start on managing time in society and will stand a better chance of not re-offending because *"The one who is in you is greater than the one who is in the world"* (1 John 4:4). That inmate (soon to be ex-offender) has hope and a future. *"For in this hope we were saved. But hope that is seen is no hope at all. Who hopes for what he already has? But if we hope for what we do not yet have, we wait for it patiently"* (Romans 8:24-25).

Although believers have not yet fully received all the blessings of salvation and eternal life that God has promised us when Christ's new Kingdom is established, we can face each new day with hope and look forward to spending eternity with our Creator. In the meantime, we're admonished to *"Be very careful, then, how you live, not as unwise but as wise, making the most of every opportunity, because the days are evil"* (Ephesians 5:15-16). Managing time is a perfect way to do that. Let hope be your motivator.

> **"God... instructs us and teaches us how to be faithful and effective stewards (managers) of the time He gives us by giving us something real to be hopeful for each day."**

God gives us this hope each day and confirms His promise to us of salvation and eternal life throughout His Word. In it He instructs us and teaches us how to be faithful and effective stewards (managers) of the time He gives us by giving us something real to be hopeful for each day. A perfect example of this is found in His Word in John 3:16. Most of you reading this book are already familiar with this passage of Scripture. But for those who are not, Jesus says *"For God so loved the world that he gave his one and only Son, that whoever believes in him shall not perish but have eternal life."* In the very next verse, He says *"For God did not send his Son into the world to condemn the world, but to save the world through Him"* (John 3:17). That is real hope, the kind you can believe and rely on.

So, do not despair while you are incarcerated; *there is hope!* If you are a believer, you already have this hope and have a better chance of managing time each day because Christ is your hope. If you are not a believer, you too can have this hope and learn how to manage time. All you have to do is *"Confess with your mouth, 'Jesus is Lord', and believe in your heart that God raised him from the dead, and you will be saved. For it is with your heart that you believe and are justified, and it is with your mouth that you confess and are saved"* (Romans 10:9-10). Jesus confirms this in Revelation 3:20, when He says *"Here I am! I stand at the door and knock. If anyone hears my voice and opens the door, I will come in and eat with him, and he with me".*

If you are an unbeliever and would like to accept Christ as your Savior and Lord, it is as simple as asking a believer at your facility to pray with you. You can also go to the last section of this chapter and pray the "Sinner's Prayer" there. This is the best investment of time you will ever make in your entire life; one that will have both earthly and eternal dividends. It is also the most important decision you will ever make in your entire life; one that has earthly and eternal implications. It has certainly been for me. I found hope when I thought all hope was lost. I found it when I accepted Christ as my Savior and Lord; He gave me the hope I needed. Once I had it, there was no letting go.

The amount of time that you invest cultivating this important spiritual attribute will determine how effective you will be at having it, not only during your incarceration, but also when you are released from prison. It is then that you will need it in full measure to make a successful transition into society, and avoid reoffending. Serve time productively. Keep hope alive!

LOVE

Love can be defined in many different ways. But what exactly is love? The Bible says, *"God is love"* (1 John 4:16). You might ask, *"How does God love us"*? *"This is how God showed his love among us: He sent his one and only Son into the world that we might live through him. This is love: not that we loved God, but that he loved us and sent his Son as an atoning sacrifice for our sins"* (1 John 4:9-10).

Mankind's definition of love and God's definition of love are two very different things. Mankind defines love as something you feel. God defines love as something you do. Unlike mankind, God's kind of love is directed outward toward others, not inward toward self. There is no place for "self" in God's kind of love.

The reason there is so much hate in the world is because there isn't enough of God's love being displayed. The correctional setting, unfortunate as it may be, is a place where hate is nothing less than a way of life. God's kind of love is practically nonexistent. Were it not for believers, love would not exist in the correctional setting. More often than not, the only time you see it is when God-fearing inmates display it. I not only witnessed hate up close and personal many times during my quarter-century of incarceration, I displayed it many times as well. When I think of all the times I allowed hate to dictate my actions toward other inmates, for reasons that are as old as prisons themselves, I realize how much time I wasted engaging in negative behavior when I could have been utilizing that time productively.

I could give you many examples of the hate I displayed towards other inmates, but that would have required me to write an entire chapter on just that subject. I would have been giving kudos to the author of hate (Satan) by doing so, not to mention the time it would have required to write a chapter dealing with just that; not exactly a productive use of time. Instead, let me give you an example of the time I invested displaying love towards other inmates once I learned how to do so God's way.

14

> *"I did not want my relationship with God to be phony, so I stopped allowing hate to dictate my actions towards fellow inmates."*

"If anyone says, 'I love God,' yet hates his brother, he is a liar. For anyone who does not love his brother, whom he has seen, cannot love God, whom he has not seen" (1 John 4:20). This passage of scripture opened my eyes to the fact that my relationship with God could not be real if I was not showing love to those around me, believers and unbelievers alike. I did not want my relationship with God to be phony, so I stopped allowing hate to dictate my actions towards fellow inmates. I made it my business to begin showing genuine love to everyone I came in contact with; that included staff members.

Was that an easy thing to do? I would be lying if I said it was. The truth is it was anything but easy. There were times when an inmate or a staff member would rub me the wrong way, for one reason or another, and I would be tempted to deal with him or her physically. I lost count of the times I had to "turn the other cheek" to avoid reacting to a situation in a physical manner. Violence was the only language I understood when I was walking in darkness.

One such incident was when an inmate who was serving two life sentences walked into the library and swung on me. I was the law clerk at the time and just happened to be in the library alone that day. Why this inmate swung on me isn't important. Suffice it to say, he simply didn't like me and was trying his hardest to get me to jeopardize my parole date (I had under five years left to serve at the time). He managed to clip me on the side of the head and I almost lost it. I jumped out of my chair immediately, and with a sharpened pencil in my hand I began walking toward him. When he realized what I was about to do, he panicked and began to apologize. The devil's a liar... and a COWARD! Had I not been sincere about walking in God's love at the time, I could have easily gotten myself into a world of trouble, and then I would have been sitting in segregation kicking myself in the rear for allowing myself to go there. Even worse, instead of being paroled when I was supposed to be, I might have ended up with another case and another sentence to serve. Talk about a setback. That would have been it...and then some!

But by the grace of God, I did not allow my "flesh" (the sinful nature we all have) to pull me off my spiritual square, and instead was able to display God's love to this inmate by not reacting physically. I believe he was trying to see if I would react the way I would have when I was gang banging. Instead, what he got was a raw dose of God's unconditional love. Did that cause him to stop hating on me? No, it didn't. What it did was show him that I was sincere about walking in God's love and that nothing or no one was going to force me to act otherwise. Other inmates that hated on me during that time got the message as well. I simply wasn't going to hate anymore. That is how I chose to manage time overall from that point forward.

A classic example of the hate most often displayed in the correctional setting has to do with the violence that occurs almost daily, whether it's gang violence, racially motivated violence, inmate-on-inmate violence, or violence against staff. At the end of the day, hate is hate no matter how you choose to define it. It is a deadly contagion that opens the door to all kinds of evil. If left unchecked, hate will keep you from serving time productively and may even cause you to prolong your stay past your parole date. Hate does what it does best, it destroys the hater!

At the beginning of each day, we must choose whether we are going to love God and others, or whether we are going to hate them. Genuine love is not a feeling. It is a choice and an action. We can choose to love or hate God and others, and even ourselves for that matter. However, we must be mindful that our choice to love or hate will have not only earthly consequences (here and now), but eternal consequences (for all of eternity) as well. We all have to stand before

God someday to give an account of how we managed the time he blessed us with (Romans 14:10-12; 2 Corinthians 5:10). Do we invest it wisely loving Him and others, or squander it hating Him and others? I cannot stress enough the importance of investing time displaying this priceless spiritual attribute on a daily basis during and after your incarceration. Your eternal destination hinges on it.

> *"The amount of time I spent hating God and others during the first eight-years of my incarceration was time I could have spent learning how to love instead."*

Not only is this the most productive way an inmate can serve time, but nothing else in the area of time management in a correctional setting is more vital. I learned this the hard way. The amount of time I spent hating God and others during the first eight-years of my incarceration was time I could have spent learning how to love instead. That, my brothers and sisters, is time I will never get back. I give thanks to God, however, because through His unconditional love, mercy, and grace, I was able to manage the remainder of my time incarcerated loving Him and others, instead of hating Him and others.

If you do not know how to love God and others, it is as easy as investing time studying His Holy Word so that He, through His Spirit, can teach you how to do so. He will instruct you and teach you in the way you should go (Psalm 32:8). Moreover, there will always be a believer at your facility who knows the Word, and he/she can teach you. God will see to it. He always does. He did that with me by sending one of His devoted servants to me when I was backslidden.

In early 1991, I was transferred to the facility where I would end up serving the remainder of the seventeen years I had left on my 48-year sentence. I had just spent the previous eight years of my incarceration lost and wandering aimlessly. Although I had been born again by accepting Christ as my Savior, I was in a terribly backslidden condition because I had allowed myself to continue in my old way of thinking, instead of "being transformed by the renewing of my mind" (Romans 12:2).

I could have easily stayed in that worldly rut had God not intervened. He did so by sending Carlos, a devoted servant of the Lord, to lead me back to Him. Carlos was a volunteer Bible study teacher who visited several prisons throughout northern and central Illinois to fellowship with inmates who were serious about learning the Word of God so they could draw into a closer relationship with Him.

When he first started coming to the facility I was housed at, I was in such a backslidden frame of mind that I really was not trying to hear what he had to say. I reasoned that if I wanted to hear someone preach to me I could always call my brother, who was an ordained pastor. After several attempts to get Carlos to quit pursuing me, including asking the Chaplain himself to tell Carlos to stop coming to my housing unit, I gave in. That was the work of the Holy Spirit. Neither God nor Carlos tried to force their will on me. Nevertheless, God was not giving up on me and neither was Carlos.

God does not force His will on anyone. However, when you give your life to Christ and do it genuinely, as I clearly did when I dedicated my life to Christ, He is not going to let you walk away just like that. John 10:28 says *"For the Lord knows those who are His and no one can snatch them out of His hand"*. This was the beginning of my quest to learn how to love God and others. As I stated previously, this was the best investment of time I ever made during my incarceration.

The Bible says in 1 John 5:3 *"This is love for God: to obey His commands. And His commands are not burdensome"*. The most important command God gave us is this: *"Love the LORD your God with all your heart and with all your soul and with all your strength"* (Deuteronomy 6:5). The second most important command is to *"Love your neighbor as yourself"* (Leviticus 19:18). God confirms His Word to us in these Old Testament scriptures when He reiterates them in the New Testament (Matthew 22:37-39).

I discovered one of the easiest ways to love God and others in a correctional setting is to invest time being mindful of the fact that *"Love is patient, love is kind. It does not envy, it does not boast, it is not proud. It is not rude, it is not self-seeking, it is not easily angered, it keeps no record of wrongs. Love does not delight in evil, but rejoices with the truth. It always protects, always trusts, always hopes, always perseveres. Love never fails. And now these three remain: faith, hope and love. But the greatest of these is love"* (1 Corinthians 13:1-8).

In sum, faith is the foundation and content of God's Word. Hope is the attitude and focus. Love is the action. When faith and hope are in line, you will find it easier to love God and others because you will have a better understanding and appreciation of how and why God loves you. *"This is love: not that we loved God, but that he loved us and sent his Son as an atoning sacrifice for our sins"* (1 John 4:10).

Faith gives substance to things we hope for. Love binds them together in perfect unity. It's not rocket science. It's a matter of doing what is right (loving others) and avoiding that which is wrong (hating others). Which will you choose? Be wise in how you answer that question. Your release date may depend on it. Mine did!

Invest time during your incarceration loving God and others, and your management of time will be a productive and rewarding experience. Do this and you will be able to speak of your time in prison as a success instead of a setback. If I was able to do this, then so can you.

PRAYER

We have already established that faith is the substance of things hoped for, hope is an anchor for the soul, and love binds them together in perfect unity. Without faith, hope and love, we cannot tap into God's

19

infinite wisdom. So how do we do this? *Through prayer!* Prayer is the key that unlocks all three. We cannot unlock one without the other. What then is prayer? Simply put, prayer is the act of communicating with God.

Next to Bible study, prayer is by far the most important spirit time-related "activity" you can engage in. We simply cannot have a relationship with God apart from it, for prayer is the only means we have of communicating with God. The Lord Jesus Christ made it possible for us to communicate directly with the Father through His sacrificial death on the cross (Romans 5:1-2 / Hebrews 4:14-16 / Hebrews 10:19).

Now that we have direct access to God through His Son Jesus Christ, we have no excuse for not appropriating that access. How do we do that? *Through prayer.* The amount of time we spend communicating with God is a measure of our devotion to Him. There is a universal principle that comes with it: You only get out of it what you put into it! The more time you invest praying, the more results you will get. Spend less time praying and you can expect minimal results. 2 Corinthians 9:6 says *"Whoever sows sparingly will also reap sparingly, and whoever sows generously will also reap generously"*.

Prayer has been made by some to be a hard, frustrating, meaningless task. Nothing could be further from the truth. If anything, prayer can be an easy, joyful, and meaningful time management activity that you can engage in daily and expect results from; not only during your incarceration, but when you reenter society as well.

It is important to remember that we will have to stand before God someday to give an account of how we managed "His" time here on Earth. I say "His" time because it's not "our" time; we are only stewards of it. That's why it is important that we manage it wisely. If you have accepted Jesus Christ as your Savior and Lord, you have no excuse for not spending time daily in prayer with God. You cannot use

> *"...prayer can be an easy, joyful, and meaningful time management activity that you can engage in daily and expect results from..."*

the excuse that you barely have time for anything, because time is all you have. Keep in mind that I was incarcerated, so I know all the excuses an inmate may give for neglecting this, that, and the other, including something as important as prayer.

Prayer cannot and should not be taken lightly. It is serious business. When we come to God in prayer we have to come correct, meaning, we have to believe He is hearing us and that our prayers are in line with His will. God's Word is His will. When we pray according to His Word, we have automatically prayed in line with His will. *"This is the confidence we have in approaching God: that if we ask anything according to his will, he hears us. And if we know that he hears us—whatever we ask—we know that we have what we asked of him"* (John 5:14-15).

God answers prayers in one of three ways: yes, no, or wait. If we pray according to His will, we can expect for our prayers to be answered "yes" every time. If we do not pray according to His will we can expect our prayers to be answered "no" every time, because God will never go against His own will and He will never contradict His Word. *"God watches over His Word to perform it"* (Jeremiah 1:12), and *"It will not return to Him empty but will accomplish what He desires and achieve the purpose for which He sent it"* (Isaiah 55:11). At times, for reasons we may not fully understand, we may have to wait for our prayers to be answered. This calls for patience. "Be still and wait patiently for the LORD" (Psalm 37:7).

In addition to the three different answers God gives to prayer, there are different types of prayer you can incorporate into your daily management of time that will aid you in making good use of this priceless spiritual activity. One is **personal** prayer (prayers you pray to

God concerning yourself); another is **intercessory** prayer (prayers on behalf of one or more people, your family, church, neighborhood, city, even the nation(s)); and another is **group** prayer or "**corporate** prayer" as it called by some (prayers prayed in a group setting, in one accord). If you incorporate any of these types of prayer in your daily management of time, you will find yourself doing exactly what the Word of God instructs us to do: *"Pray in the Spirit on all occasions with all kinds of prayers and requests"* (Ephesians 6:18), and *"Pray continually"* (1 Thessalonians 5:17).

God is not a light switch that we can turn on and off when it's convenient for us. We must stay in constant, daily communication with Him in order for our prayers to be effective and produce results (desired answers). Our prayer time must be consistent. We must guard it zealously. We must be disciplined managers of that precious time we spend in prayer.

The Bible says *"Even when we do not know how to pray... The Holy Spirit intercedes for us with groans that words cannot express"* (Romans 8:26). Therefore, those who believe in God have no excuse for not praying. If we say that we believe in God, and we're serious about the Father's business as Jesus clearly was during His time on the earth, then we should make it a point to set aside some time each day, throughout the day, to pray.

Personal Prayer
So how does one *"pray in the spirit on all occasions"* or *"pray continually?"* You can start by making, brief prayers, your response to each situation you encounter throughout the day. Another is to order your every step around God's Word so that your life becomes a prayer. You do not have to isolate yourself from others or bring whatever you are doing to a halt in order to *"pray in the spirit on all occasions"* or to *"pray continually."* You can make prayer your life and your life a prayer if you *"Devote yourselves to prayer"* (Colossians 4:2). We do this by *"Fixing our eyes on Jesus, the author and perfecter of our faith"* (Hebrews 12:2).

> *"Although managing time from a prayerful standpoint may not come easy, it is imperative if you desire to develop a close relationship with God."*

Although managing time from a prayerful standpoint may not come easy, it is imperative if you desire to develop a close relationship with God. The secret to developing this relationship (that we might tap into God's infinite wisdom to learn how to become effective time managers) is to spend time with Him each day. Certainly we cannot spend all our time praying, but we can certainly have a prayerful mindset at all times. A prayerful mindset should not be a substitute for personal times of prayer, but an extension of those times. Constant communication is vital to any relationship and is certainly necessary for building and maintaining a true and lasting relationship with God. How else can we expect to be effective time managers? I can't think of any other way. Can you?

Have you ever grown weary or disillusioned when praying for something or someone? If you are a person who prays, then you know what I'm talking about. Nevertheless, know that persistence is an expression of faith that God does answer prayer. Do not despair. God's timing is always perfect because He is the Creator and Keeper of time even though He Himself is not bound by it. His perfect answers to your persistent prayers will come at the "appointed time" (Habakkuk 2:1-3)

Your faith should not waver if the answer to your prayer comes slowly, especially if it is premised upon a promise of God in His Word. The delay (or season of waiting) may be God's way of working His perfect will in your life (Romans 4:20). So when you feel impatient or disillusioned with praying, know that God is always present, always listening, always answering, maybe not in ways you had hoped, but certainly in ways He knows best. God reassures us about this when He says, "Be still and know that I am God" (Psalm 46:10).

I am a living example that God truly answers prayer, but I first had to learn how to "be still and know that He is God." I did that by placing my trust in Him and believing that He had power to do what He promised in His Word (Romans 4:20). I have had many of my prayers answered yes, no, or wait. Those that were answered "yes" were answered that way because I prayed *"according to His will"* (1 John 5:14-15). It is when I failed to pray according to His will that my prayers were answered "no" (James 4:3). Then there were times when I simply had to *"be still and wait patiently for Him"* (Psalm 37:7). That called for *perseverance* (James 1:3-4).

Patience is one of those things that every believer must learn to develop in order to fully trust in God's timing, especially where it concerns prayer. I certainly had to. And if it worked for me, it will work for you. All you have to do is let go and let God.

Do you have a regular time to pray? If not, try to set aside a specific time that you can commit (morning, noon, or night) to get alone with the Father. If you're an early riser, that is the best time to pray because your mind is more at peace and you can spend quality time in the Father's presence. You can also commit the entire day to Him. You can begin your morning prayer like this: *"In the morning, O' LORD you hear my voice; in the morning I lay my requests before you and wait in expectation"* (Psalm 5:3).

Consider the following quote from Andrew Murray, a South African writer, teacher and Christian pastor: *"Many think that they must, with their defective spiritual life, work themselves up to pray more. They do not understand that only in proportion as the spiritual life is strengthened can the prayer life increase. Prayer and life are inseparably connected."*

Intercessory Prayer
As I stated previously, intercessory prayer is done on behalf of others, your church, neighborhood, city, or nations. God exhorts us to be intercessors (1 Timothy 2:1-4). There are many examples of intercessory

prayer found throughout the Bible. Suffice it to say, if you believe in God, then it is your duty as a believer to spend time interceding for fellow believers and whomever else the Spirit of the Lord impresses upon you to pray for (Ephesians 6:18).

> *"Intercessory prayer causes the Spirit of God to move mightily in the Earth."*

Intercessory prayer causes the Spirit of God to move mightily in the Earth. Because of the critical time we live in, the Holy Spirit is calling on all believers everywhere to invest time interceding. Look around you. There are a number of people or places you can intercede for. Invest time sowing seeds of prayer into someone else's life. *"For at the proper time we will reap a harvest if we do not give up"* (Galatians 6:9). *"The prayer of a righteous man is powerful and effective"* (James 5:16). Intercessory prayer is a wise use of time!

Group Prayer
If you are housed in the same cell-house and on the same wing with other believers and there currently is no group prayer time, I encourage you to come together in agreement to set aside a specific time to pray together each day. I used to do this with other Christian brothers I was incarcerated with. We would meet in the day room of our housing unit just before lock-up each day. We would form a prayer circle, hold hands, and take turns praying aloud. We chose that specific time because it gave us an opportunity as a group to give God thanksgiving and praise for helping us live through another day of incarceration, despite the difficult circumstances we faced each day.

Whatever time of day you choose to pray together or wherever you choose to meet (i.e., day room, chapel, yard, gym, etc.), the important thing is that you meet each day, if possible. This is an excellent time to *agree in prayer* (Matthew 18:19) about issues that are near and dear to your heart, and is another form of *fellowship* (Hebrews 10:25). You will be honoring God by being faithful *stewards* (managers) of that precious time spent together in prayer. Make good use of your time while incarcerated by making prayer your life and your life a prayer. You will be serving time as productively as anyone can in a correctional setting.

Prayer for Salvation

As a Christian, it is my duty to share my faith with unbelievers, to show them what God has done in my life, and to ask if they would like to accept Jesus Christ as their Savior and Lord. If you are an unbeliever and would like to accept Jesus Christ as your Savior and Lord, please pray the following:

> *Lord Jesus, I know I am a sinner in need of salvation. I am tired of living my life the world's way and I am ready to begin living it your way. I repent of every sin I have ever commited against you in thought, word, and deed. I ask you, Lord Jesus, to forgive me, deliver me, cleanse me, and heal me from all my sins with your precious blood. Come into my life and save me, Lord Jesus, for I confess with my mouth that you are Lord, and I believe with my heart that God raised you from the dead. I surrender my life to you this day and ask you to help me live for you every day from this day forward. In your precious and Holy Name, I pray. Amen.*

If you prayed that prayer, you have just made the most important decision of your life. Know that there are angels in Heaven rejoicing over you and glorifying God at this very moment (Luke 15:7). Feel free to write me at the address listed at the press page of this book to let me know you prayed that prayer, so that I too can rejoice over you in the Lord for your salvation. You now are a child of God, according to John 1:12. As such, you belong to the family of God (John 1:12; Ephesians 3:14)) and have covenant rights according to Galatians 3:26-29. Get with other believers who are genuine about their walk with God and let them disciple you.

Once you are established and confident in your relationship with the Lord, you can exercise your faith by letting Him lead you to others who need salvation and follow-up discipleship. *"Therefore go and make disciples of all nations, baptizing them in the name of the Father and of the Son and of the Holy Spirit, and teaching them to obey everything I have commanded you. And surely I am with you always, to the very end of the age"* (Matthew 28:19-20).

The Lord's Prayer

"Our Father in heaven, hallowed be your name, your kingdom come, your will be done on earth as it is in heaven. Give us our daily bread. Forgive us our debts, as we also have forgiven our debtors. And lead us not into temptation, but deliver us from the evil one" (MATTHEW 6:9-13). This is a good "model" for prayer that the Lord Jesus gave us (I personally like the King James Version better). Use it. Expound on it. God is listening!

FASTING

This is one of those areas of managing Spirit Time that I lament not having invested more time applying while incarcerated. Why? Because it would have enabled me to draw nearer to God (James 4:8) and to strengthen my relationship with Him by making me even more dependent on Him. Apart from Him, we can do nothing (John 15;5), but through Him we can do all things because He strengthens us (Philippians 4:13). Moreover, I would have been even more disciplined at applying all of the other equally important Biblical disciplines mentioned in this book. Not only while incarcerated, but moreso, when I made the challenging transition from prison back to society. Fasting would have enabled me to move forward at a higher level with God a lot sooner. Shouldn't that be the desire of every true believer--to be at a higher level with God? It is for me, and it should be for you too, if you truly love Jesus. But just as with every other time management-related discipline written in this book, you only get out of fasting what you put into it.

If you're wondering why I didn't apply this Biblical discipline more often during my incarceration, it's because I didn't discipline myself to do it. My loss, someone else's gain. But because I don't spend time focusing on could've, would've, should've--except to learn from my mistakes so that I never repeat them--I'm not going to spend any more time writing about why I didn't. Suffice it to say, I fast now and benefit from it in every way that a true believer should.

That said, I'm writing about fasting to encourage and equip you to invest time applying it during your incarceration (if you aren't doing so already), so that you can consecrate yourself before the Lord Jesus Christ and receive all the benefits [rewards] that come with it. This will help you to become disciplined at making it a consistent part of your relationship with God both during and after your incarceration, and help you to be disciplined and consistent in each of the five areas this book covers. Fasting is the most powerful--and one of the most difficult to undertake--of all other Christian disciplines. Try it, if you haven't already; you will not be disappointed, but you will be abundantly blessed. It's God's promise! (Psalm 5:12; 128:1-2).

Be mindful that fasting has to do with the condition of your heart, and not with how long you fast. Here are several reasons why you should fast:

1. Fasting will cause you to draw near to God, so that He can draw near to you (this is the goal of fasting); (James 4:8).

2. Fasting will cause you to become more dependent on the Lord by going without food for a designated period of time (John 15:5).

3. Fasting is a Biblical way to humble yourself before God (Psalm 35:13).

4. Fasting reinforces your feelings of repentance and reminds

you not only of your human weakness, but also of your dependence upon God (2 Chronicles 20:9,12).

5. Fasting enables the Holy Spirit to reveal your true spiritual condition, resulting in brokenness, repentance, and a transformed life (Romans 7:14-25).

6. Fasting can transform your prayer life into a deeper and more personal experience (Daniel 9:3).

7. Fasting can result in a dynamic personal revival in your life (Psalm 85:4-7), and make you a channel of revival to others who are broken and hurting (2 Corinthians 1:3-7).

The most important thing to do before you undertake any fast is to be prayerful about which fast to undertake and to be precise about why you're doing it, being mindful that fasting is about the condition of the heart, and not the number of days that you fast. The following are four types of fasts to consider:

1. Total Fast- This absolute type of fasting calls for complete obedience and dependence upon God, so DO NOT try to undertake it unless you are certain that you are being led by the Holy Spirit (Matthew 4:1-2), and receive specific instructions from Him (Psalm 32;8) regarding how many days to do this type of fast, whether 3-days, 10-days, 3-weeks, or 40-days (Daniel 1:12, 10:3; Acts 9:9; Deuteronomy 9:9; 1 Kings 19:8). Abstain from eating food (solid or liquid) and from drinking anything, including water. If you choose to undertake this type of fasting, stay encouraged, for God will never lead you where His Word cannot take you.

2. Daniel Fast - This type of fast requires eating vegetables only and drinking water only, and/or abstaining from choice food, i.e., delicacies, and no meat or wine (Daniel 1:12; 10:3). Assuming you don't drink homemade wine (hootch), you would want to abstain from drinking

anything but water.

3. Partial Fast - This type of fast can be done from sun-up to sundown, or during specific times of the day. Also known as the Jewish Fast, it involves not eating any type of food in the morning or afternoon, i.e., 6:00 a.m.-3:00 p.m. You can, however, drink water, juice, or other liquids during the fasting period.

4. Soul Fast - This type of fast is recommended [only as a starting point] for those who don't have experience fasting or who have never fasted; for those with health concerns that might prevent them from abstaining from food, water or other dietary elements; or for those that desire to readjust certain areas of their life that might need change (Deuteronomy 30:6; Isaiah 58:3; Romans 12:1-2; Galatians 5:1, 16-17; Hebrews 12:1-12). If this is you, an example would be if you have access to your own TV or radio — as I did when I was incarcerated — that you desire to stop watching secular TV programs that promote the things of this world instead of Christ, stop listening to music that doesn't edify you or glorify God, or abstain from activities at your facility that cause you to spend more time engaged in those activities than in doing the things that draw you near to God, i.e., praying, studying and meditating on the Word of God, fellowshipping with other believers, encouraging other inmates that are hurting

Remember, the length of any fast should never overshadow the purpose of the fast, and especially the condition of your heart prior to the fast. Ask God to reveal any area in your life that needs change and be willing and obedient to change it (Isaiah 1:19). Be encouraged and let the strength of your focus be on the Lord Jesus Christ. Selah!

BIBLE STUDY
In Christianity, Bible study is *the study of the Bible by ordinary people*

> *"One of the best ways to develop faith in God is to spend quality time studying the Bible."*

as a personal, religious, or spiritual practice. Some denominations may call this *devotion* or *devotional acts*; however, in other denominations *devotion* has other meanings. Bible study in this sense is distinct from *biblical studies*, which is a *formal academic discipline*.

Personal Bible Study

One of the best ways to develop faith in God is to spend quality time studying the Bible. There is no better way to know God than through His Word. The Bible (Basic Instructions Before Leaving Earth) reveals to us who God is (i.e., his character, nature, and will). Spending time searching the Scriptures, meditating on them, and making them part of your prayers is a valuable and beneficial use of time because it brings us into a closer, deeper, and more meaningful relationship with our Creator (John 15:4-5).

We learn to know who God is and how to walk with Him by studying, meditating on, and praying His Word. That means setting aside time each day to read, study, and think about (meditate on) the things God reveals to us through His Word. It is how we nourish our spirit. Just as the body needs food and water to sustain it physically, our spirit needs spiritual nourishment, too. The Word of God is the spiritual food that sustains us and keeps us from dying of spiritual hunger and thirst (John 4:13-14; 6:27, 32-35, 48-51, 58). Jesus, who is the Word of God (John 1:14 / Hebrews 1:2), offers Himself as the "spiritual bread" from Heaven that satisfies completely and leads to eternal life (John 6:32-35).

We must keep in mind that the Bible is not a textbook, storybook, or history book. It is life's instruction manual. It is the very wisdom of God Almighty written down so that we can apply it to everyday circumstances. When we invest time daily in the Word, that investment pays off in every area of our lives. The dividend that this investment pays is not just eternal, but is also for here and now. Just as there are heavenly rewards for living right before God, there are also earthly rewards. It is up to each individual Christian to appropriate these blessings. The Word of God gives you instructions on how exactly to do this.

Studying and meditating the Word of God is the first step toward applying it to our everyday lives (Joshua 1:8). The more knowledge you have of God's Word, the more wisdom and understanding you will have to guide you in your daily decisions. *"For the LORD gives wisdom, and from His mouth come knowledge and understanding"* (Proverbs 2:6). You will know how to live your life daily according to God's purpose and will, which will make serving time meaningful and productive and give you a head-start on making a successful transition in society when you are released. That is exactly what the Word of God did for me. Now I am able to *"Show myself as one approved, a workman who does not need to be ashamed and who correctly handles the word of truth"* (2 Timothy 2:15).

Bible study can be done on your own time (personal Bible study) or in a group setting (group Bible study). Both are equally important and beneficial to your spiritual growth. Just as you should set aside a specific time to pray on a daily basis, you should have a specific time each day to read, study, and meditate on the truths that you learn from the Bible as well. Your personal study time should be free from distractions like TV or radio. If you have a "celly" (cellmate) who doesn't share your belief in God, doesn't pray or read the Bible, then respectfully come to an understanding with him/her regarding your

> *"Just as you should set aside a specific time to pray daily, you should have a specific time each day to read, study, meditate on, and pray the truths that you learn from the Bible."*

personal Bible study time by asking him/her to allow you that time free from distractions and noise.

If you do not know how to study the Bible, buy yourself a study Bible or ask a family member, relative, etc. to buy you one. A good study Bible should come with extensive footnotes on Bible verses, personality profiles, book introductions, outlines, Harmony of the Gospels, maps, charts and diagrams, cross-references, textual notes and sectional headings, an index, and a dictionary/concordance. I bought a *Life Application Study Bible* when I was incarcerated and it made my personal and group Bible study a time to look forward to.

My *Life Application Study Bible*, with the aid of the Holy Spirit, helped increase my knowledge and understanding of God's Word one-hundred fold. I still have that Bible, and I read, study, meditate, pray, and do my best to *act* on its truths daily. In doing so, I am like the one who receives the seed that falls on good soil. I hear the Word, understand it, and act on it, therefore, I produce a crop that yields thirty, sixty, and even a hundred-times what was sown (Matthew 13:23 / Matthew 7:24-26). You can, too.

As for translations, you must decide for yourself which one suits you best, be it the King James Version (KJV), New King James Version (NKJV), New American Standard Bible (NASB), New International Version (NIV), Amplified (AMP), New Living Translation (NLT), Message, (MSG), etc. I have studied each translation and have found the NIV the easiest to understand. If you do not have a Bible and decide to get one, ask the Holy Spirit to guide you in making your choice of translation.

Group Bible Study
Personal Bible study time should motivate you to attend Group Bible study as often as possible during your incarceration. I doubt there is a correctional facility (state or federal, jail or prison) in this country that doesn't have one or more Bible study groups that meet at least once

per week. The exception would be lockdown facilities (i.e., Supermax, and/or maximum security facilities that have limited programs due to security concerns). If you are fortunate enough to be in a correctional facility that is not on permanent lockdown or one with limited programs, and there are group Bible studies taking place, I encourage you to take full advantage of that opportunity if you have not already.

The Bible says that fellowship is vital to one's relationship with God and fellow believers (Hebrews 10:19-25). By attending group Bible study you will be doing what Hebrews 10:25 says: *"Let us not give up meeting, as some are in the habit of doing, but let us encourage one another, and all the more as you see the day approaching."* You attend group Bible study for the purpose of fellowship, to seek God with your brothers or sisters-in-Christ, and to learn truths of the Bible from other fellow believers who are more knowledgeable of God's Word than you are (Matthew 18:20; I John 1:1-4).

Be mindful during your personal and group Bible study time that the Bible is the inerrant and irrefutable Word of God and should be studied and followed with the utmost sincerity. *"For the Word of God is living and active. Sharper than any double-edged sword, it penetrates even to dividing soul and spirit, joints and marrow; it judges the thoughts and attitudes of the heart"* (Hebrews 4:12). Not only is the Bible living and active, it is life-changing and dynamic as it works in us.

With the careful incision of a surgeon's knife, God's Word reveals who and what we are. It digs deep into the moral and spiritual center of our innermost being and discerns what is within us, both good and bad. It gives us instruction on how to live our lives in a manner that is holy and pleasing to God. Our part is to be obedient to the Holy Spirit so that He can teach us all things and remind us of everything Jesus said to us in His Word.

Personal and group Bible studies are productive time management activities because you are focused on doing something positive and beneficial during that time. You are sowing seed on good soil and will reap a bountiful harvest, both in this life and in the one to come. The God of the universe personally guarantees it (Psalm 1:1-3; Revelation 21:6-7). Be disciplined and consistent with your personal and group Bible study time, and you will find yourself serving time productively.

CHAPEL ACTIVITIES

Not only is the chapel a positive environment to spend time at in a correctional setting, but participating in chapel-related activities is one of the most productive ways to manage time while incarcerated. If you are serious about your relationship with God and desire to manage time productively, I encourage you to get involved in as many chapel-related activities as possible during your incarceration. This will help you to *"...set your mind on things above..."* (Colossians 3:1), and draw you closer to the Lord that He may draw closer to you (James 4:8).

If the chapel department at your facility has a job opening for "Chapel Clerk," consider putting in a request for it. The time you will spend clerking for the chaplain will be time served productively, because you will be serving God, not man, right where you are.

Also, for those of you who are going to be released, I encourage you to find a Bible-based church in the community where you plan to reside, particularly one that has a prison ministry geared toward helping ex-offenders to make a successful transition in society. This is one of the most effective ways to avoid reoffending. It is also an effective way to manage time in society.

I can attest to this, because being a committed servant of the Kingdom of God at my church has helped me mature spiritually and keeps me on the straight and narrow path, the one that leads to justice, mercy and faith. I know in my heart that I will NEVER reoffend, because I have no desire to reoffend. I am committed to helping *decrease* the recidivism rate. That is one of the purposes for this book. I shall not waiver in that commitment!

THOUGHT PROVOKERS
Chapter One: Spirit Time

1. Prayer is the only means of communicating with God. How much time do you invest praying? _____
   _____
   _____
   _____

2. Faith is the substance of things _____ for, the evidence of things not_____.

3. Personal and group bible study are important time management activities. If you invest time doing one or both, what returns are you seeing on the time you've invested so far? _____
   _____
   _____
   _____

4. Why is hope such an important spiritual attribute to invest time cultivating?_____
   _____

5. Mankind's definition of love and God's definition of love are two very different things. How do you define love? _____
   _____
   _____

> *If you are not currently attending chapel activities, I'd like to encourage you to go the next time chapel line is called on your wing. Invest however much time you're allowed to be there just listening to whoever is speaking. Then reflect on what you heard throughout the rest of the week and see if you can apply any of it.*

-Two-

SOUL TIME

"Instruct a wise man and he will be wiser still; teach a righteous man and he will add to his learning." - **Proverbs 9:9**

Now that you have read how important it is to invest time feeding your spirit during your incarceration, let us examine how important it is to invest time feeding your soul, aka, the mind. The two are inseparably connected.

I believe a spiritual battle is being waged for the souls of mankind. Who can deny it? Certainly not anyone who is incarcerated! I could not deny this spiritual reality during my incarceration and neither could others I did time with. My mind gravitated toward negativity more times than not before I rededicated my life to Christ and learned how to manage time. Once I did learn how to manage time I was able to resist allowing myself to engage in unproductive activity. This enabled me to move forward, achieve goals, and thereby serve time as productively as one can in a correctional setting.

When an inmate's mind is on idle mode it is not being productive. That is a mind which is vulnerable and predisposed to negative thoughts. The inmate who is serious about managing time will not allow his mind to become idle. By investing time daily feeding your mind with productive thoughts, you will be less prone to engage in unproductive activity. The best way to do this is to follow Paul's instruction and take captive *every* thought to make it obedient to Christ (2 Corinthians 10:5).

As someone who spent a considerable amount of time engaging in the following productive activities while incarcerated, and who benefitted immensely from them as a result, I encourage you to engage in these activities as well. They will keep your mind from becoming idle and will help you become an efficient time manager.

EDUCATION

If you were not fortunate enough to graduate from high school and currently do not have a G.E.D., I encourage you to take advantage of the opportunity you still have during your incarceration to obtain it. If you are within two years of your release date, you still have ample time to study and learn what you need to know to take the G.E.D. test and, hopefully, pass it. If you still have more than two years left to serve, then you have no excuse not to obtain your G.E.D. Invest the time and just do it!

> *"The criminal justice system can incarcerate your body but it cannot incarcerate your mind unless YOU allow it to."*

If you are in a lockdown facility that does not offer Adult Basic Education courses, there are correspondence courses you can take (ask your counselor if he or she can provide you with that information). Do not allow a prison cell to deter you from achieving such a noble goal. The criminal justice system can incarcerate your body but it cannot incarcerate your mind unless YOU allow it to. Once you have your G.E.D. in hand, you will be glad you got it. The time that you invest studying and preparing yourself to take the G.E.D. test will yield valuable returns. I know this because I encouraged and equipped inmates during my incarceration to obtain their G.E.Ds. Soon after they achieved that goal, their entire attitude toward managing time, and more importantly, their lives in general, completely changed.

The time I invested helping these guys to obtain their G.E.D's. yielded me profitable returns by way of the writing projects I was working on at the time, projects I believe I was able to complete because of the help I provided them. God promises that he who refreshes (helps, blesses) others will himself be refreshed (Proverbs 11:25b).

If you do not have a G.E.D., then what are you waiting for? Get busy! After you achieve this goal, you should be ready to begin taking college classes and/or vocational courses and advance your education to the next level. You have nothing to lose and everything to gain. You will be serving time productively. That is your immediate reward!

Academic

I was fortunate enough to graduate from high school, despite all the madness I was caught up in during those four years. But I dropped the ball after I graduated by not taking advantage of the opportunity I had to enroll in college. My dad offered to pay the full tuition. I should have taken advantage of that opportunity. But I did not. I chose instead to continue down the dead-end road I had been traveling on since the age of twelve. At age nineteen I lost my freedom as a result.

The day I was arrested, I told my mother I was going to the police station to see what they wanted to question me about, although I already knew what it was for. I told her I would be back in a few hours, as I always did when the police asked me to come to the station to answer questions about some crime they believed I was involved in. The only difference this time was that I did not come back in a few hours. In fact, this time I did not come back for the next twenty-four years! I ended up in prison instead of enrolling in college. You snooze, you lose. I lost big-time.

During my first year of incarceration, I decided to take advantage of the academic opportunities that were available to me. With three-and-a-half years left to serve on the eight-year sentence I was serving at the time, I had more than enough time to earn an Associate's degree and to be halfway through earning a Bachelor's degree before I was paroled. The latter part of those plans never materialized.

I may have started serving my initial prison term determined to do good, but I was still "straddling the fence". In other words, I was holding on to my past while trying to move forward, not realizing the two do not mix. When you hold on to your past long enough, it will eventually catch up to you, sometimes in the worst kind of way. That is what happened to me.

I thought I was done having to deal with police, prosecutors and judges, but I was wrong. I was indicted for murder that same year (1985) and was remanded back to the Cook County Jail to await trial. I was guilty as charged, but instead of accepting the plea deal the prosecutors offered me (twenty years running concurrent with the eight years I was serving), I rolled the dice and picked a jury. Huge mistake! After a week long trial, I was convicted. The jury's verdict was unanimous: GUILTY ON ALL COUNTS!!!

Thirty-days later, I was sentenced to forty years. Ouch! That sentence ran *consecutive* to my eight-year sentence. My parole date went from March 15, 1988 to March 15, 2008, thanks to my stubbornness. I actually thought I could beat the system. That is what happens when you play with fire; *you always get burned!* I made an already stressful situation a lot more stressful by doing this, not only for myself, but for my family as well.

I then wasted the following eight years doing nothing but digging a deeper hole for myself. I simply did not care about anything anymore. It is easy to develop that type of mindset when you are serving that much prison time, but I would advise you against it. I know because

I allowed it to happen to me during those first eight years of my incarceration. That was eight years of mismanaged time!

"God had awesome plans for my life, plans to prosper me and not to harm me, plans to give me hope and a future."

Fortunately, I woke up from that mindless stupor when I did, because this book would not have been written and I would not be where I am in life today, had I not. God had awesome plans for my life, plans to prosper me and not to harm me, plans to give me hope and a future (Jeremiah 29:11). I consider myself a spiritual work in progress (Philippians 1:6). If you have Christ in your life, you are too. All believers are.

Despite having mismanaged the first eight years of my incarceration, I managed to flip the script and earn an Associate's degree because I invested the time and disciplined myself to do it. That was a huge achievement for me and a rewarding one as well. My family was able to attend the graduation ceremony and watch me receive my degree in a cap and gown. That is an experience I will never forget. I will also never forget those eight years I mismanaged. They will always serve as a reminder that time is precious and must be managed wisely whether you are incarcerated or not.

I recounted all that to say this: Once you obtain your G.E.D., do not stop there. Move forward by enrolling in college courses (if academics are your thing) and work hard toward obtaining an Associate's Degree. If the facility you are housed at offers Bachelors and Master's Degree programs, do not allow those opportunities to pass you by. Be wise and capitalize on them. Once you have those degrees you will be glad you did. Had the Illinois Department of Corrections still offered Bachelors and Master's Degree programs at its prisons when I was incarcerated, I would have obtained both. In fact, I would have walked out of prison with a Ph.D. had I been given the opportunity to do so. Although I didn't obtain a doctorate, you can if you have the opportunity to do so.

> *"Take advantage of the opportunity you have to obtain a college degree during your incarceration. It is a productive way to manage time."*

Take advantage of the opportunity you have to obtain a college degree during your incarceration. It is a productive way to manage time. Besides, you will benefit immensely by having a college degree when you are paroled because you will have marketable skills that will substantially increase your chances of getting a decent paying job. Redeem the time. Get a degree.

Vocational

If you are a "hands-on" kind of person as opposed to an academic type, and the facility you are housed at offers vocational trade programs, you should invest time taking advantage of those programs. Find out what is offered, evaluate which trade might interest you, make your choice and get yourself enrolled, even if there is a waiting list. This is one of those opportunities that are worth the wait. Any vocational trade you take and receive a Certificate of Completion or Diploma in can lead to a rewarding career in society. An employer will be more inclined to hire you if you have the skills needed to fill a particular job. You will greatly increase your chances of getting hired by having those skills.

Of course, you will need a high school diploma or a G.E.D. to enroll in a vocational trade program just as you would to take college courses. So again, if you do not have a high school diploma, invest the time that is necessary to obtain your G.E.D. should be a priority. Since all of this is general knowledge in a correctional facility, and you probably already know these things, the point then is to invest time using this knowledge to your advantage (if you haven't already).

WORK DETAIL

If you did not have a good work ethic prior to your incarceration, now is a good time to invest time establishing one. *"If a man does not work, then neither shall he eat"* (2 Thessalonians 3:10). If the premise upon which that Scripture is based was enforced by all corrections departments, there would not be an idle soul in any jail or prison anywhere in America.

Some corrections departments (like the one I served time in) have what is commonly referred to as "unassigned status", meaning an offender, in some instances, can choose not to work or attend academic or vocational programs and still receive a stipend each month. I never understood or agreed with the logic behind that, even during the eight years I mismanaged during my incarceration. If I did not do anything else that was positive during that time, I always made sure I had a work detail at each of the correctional facilities I served time at, if for no other reason, because having a work detail allowed me more movement within the facility.

Everyone who has the misfortune of being incarcerated should be required to work or attend academic or vocational programs, particularly inmates who have never done either of these things prior to their incarceration. No inmate, regardless of gender or age, should be allowed to remain unassigned and be compensated for it. Idleness breeds negativity. Negativity breeds trouble.

Some corrections departments require inmates to work but do not pay them. I do not understand or agree with the logic behind that either, nor would I ever advocate it. If an inmate is required to work, then he or she should be fairly compensated. However, whether or not you are paid for a work detail is not the issue here. The issue is that you should work if you are physically able to. Why? Work is a productive way to manage time during your incarceration. If you are not paid to work, you can pay yourself by establishing or strengthening your work ethic. In either case, you come out on top, which is a good thing in the near-term (during your incarceration) and in the long-term (when you re-enter society).

If you can get assigned to one of your facility's maintenance or correctional industry work details, you can learn a skill set tuition free and use those skills to land yourself an apprenticeship in that particular field when you're released. Even if those coveted work details are filled, you should ask to be placed on their waiting list. This is one of those "worth waiting for" opportunities.

In the meantime, you should try to land a work detail that will enable you to learn a skill that will enhance your employment prospects when you are released. Always think of both the near-term and long-term benefits. I made a priority to do that during my incarceration. The near-term benefit was being able to learn many new skill sets while incarcerated; the long-term benefit was being able to utilize those skills sets in society.

> *"There are a number of skills you can acquire in a correctional facility that can improve your employment prospects when you are released."*

There are a number of skills you can acquire in a correctional facility that can improve your employment prospects when you are released. Never limit your options. Find out what you are good at or passionate about, and then do it. If you need guidance ask the assignment placement officer or your counselor what work details are available. Perhaps they can help steer you to the work detail of your choosing or something close to it. Who knows, you might even be fortunate enough to land a work detail in the highly-coveted correctional industries at your facility (if one exists) and earn good money. Again, do not limit your options. There are marketable skills you can learn in correctional industries, facilities maintenance, dietary, print shop, commissary, warehouse, leisure time services (LTS), chapel, library, outside grounds crew, or porter work details. Keep your ear to the wire for openings in these work details, and when one opens up put in your bid.

> *"When you invest time being a genuine friend to a fellow inmate, you show that person the very heart of God."*

Rest assured that when you invest a portion of your day "earning your keep" (working) you are serving time productively. It does not matter whether you are soon to be released, still have years left to serve, or are a lifer. The benefit of working during your incarceration is one and the same for every inmate: *you learn a skill set you can use during your incarceration, and then in society when you are released.*

The Bible says *"Whatever you do, work at it with all your heart, as working for the Lord, not for men, since you know that you will receive an inheritance from the Lord as a reward. It is the Lord you are serving"* (Colossians 3:23-24). The Bible contains wisdom to guide us in the everyday things we do, including having a work detail while incarcerated. So, when you are faithful to God with a work detail, He will see to it that you are blessed and highly favored with prison officials. Read Genesis 39:20-23, and see how God did that for Joseph. If He did it for Joseph, and He did for me, He will do it for you. All you have to do is be *"willing and obedient and you will eat the best of the land"* (Isaiah 1:19a).

Since the creation of mankind, God has given us work to do. He instructed Adam when He placed him in the Garden of Eden to *"work it and take care of it"* (Genesis 2:15). If we do our work with a cheerful and grateful attitude, it becomes an act of worship, or service, to God. Such an attitude makes work, even in a correctional setting, purposeful and enjoyable. It also keeps work from becoming monotonous or boring. In a correctional setting, and especially in society, this is very important.

You should, therefore, work during and after incarceration without complaining, and regard your work as a blessing from God. By honoring God with our work, we honor Him with our time. When we honor God with our time, He rewards us with a fresh, exciting and worthwhile perspective on life. Yes, even in a correctional setting.

I know this because God did it for me during my incarceration. It is what motivated me to serve time productively by *"working at everything I did with all my heart"*, and turned what could have been a negative into a positive. If that moves you even slightly, let it be your motivation to invest time working wholeheartedly at everything you do during your incarceration. You will be turning a negative into a positive by making time serve you instead of you serving it.

COMPUTER LITERACY

Basic computer skills are a must-have in our fast-paced, technologically advanced society. You need to have these skills in order to land most decent paying jobs these days. If you are going to be released sometime in the next two to five years, I strongly advise you to take a computer course at your facility (if such courses are offered) and learn everything you can about computers, particularly data processing.

> *"When you invest time cultivating your skill, talent or gift, you honor the Creator and manage time productively during your incarceration."*

This is a good investment of time when serving time, one that will benefit you in many ways when you are released, particularly if you apply for a job that requires you to use a computer, which most jobs do nowadays. The computer skills that you acquire during your incarceration will greatly improve your employment prospects when you are released and will enable you to stay informed and current on a host of other issues you will be dealing with (i.e., family, church, housing, food, transportation, etc.).

CULTIVATE YOUR SKILLS, TALENTS, GIFTS

Everyone has a skill, talent or gift. Some people are blessed with all three. God has blessed you with one or the other, or all three. When you invest time cultivating that skill, talent or gift, you honor the Creator and manage time productively during your incarceration. If you paint, draw, write, sing, act, build, cook, teach, mentor, etc., invest time each day cultivating that skill, talent or gift with whatever resources you have available to you at your facility. The benefit to you during your incarceration will speak for itself when you reenter society.

You know the saying: USE IT OR LOSE IT! Use the skills, talents or gifts that God has blessed you with, during your incarceration, in a positive manner, and when you are released you will be more inclined to follow that path. The opportunities and rewards for doing so are many. God will present those opportunities to you and He will see to it that you are rewarded.

Every time I speak about something in this book that God can and will do for you, I speak from experience because He did these things for me during my incarceration and continues to do these things for me today, in society. The Lord blessed me with several skills, talents and gifts (e.g., writer, barber, cook, law clerk, facilities maintenance, exhorter and entrepreneur). These are things he revealed to me during my incarceration and I made sure to cultivate each one so that I would be able to utilize them upon my release. I have been able to do just that because I prepared myself in advance. That is why I encourage you to invest time during your incarceration cultivating your skills, talents or gifts so that when you are released, you will be prepared to utilize them in society. Remember: USE IT OR LOSE IT!

If you do not have a clue as to what your skills, talents or gifts are, you can always ask God to lead you to other inmates, or even staff members, who may be able to assist you in identifying what your skills, talents or gifts might be. If you still cannot identify what they are, go back to the Source. God knows better than anyone what your skills, talents or gifts are because He gave them to you (read Psalm 139:1-18). Invest your time wisely in this by going directly to Him *first* in prayer. Then search the Scriptures. You will be surprised at how quickly you will find the answers.

Most correctional facilities have arts and crafts, and culinary arts programs. If you can get into either or both I encourage you to do so. You will be surprised at how many things you can learn that you can use in a number of ways both during and after your incarceration (like everything else I write about in this book). I enrolled in both of these programs during my incarceration.

Arts and crafts taught me how to sew, a skill I was able to use many times, particularly when my clothes needed alterations. As for culinary arts, I learned how to cook better through this program and was able to use that skill when I worked in Dietary (the kitchen) at the facility I was housed at. I have also been able to use both my arts and crafts and culinary arts skills on more than one occasion in society.

As for my writing skill, you will read in Chapter five how I acquired it. Remember, God blessed you with a skill, talent or gift. Invest time now to discover what it is and then put it to use. Be a good steward of that which God has entrusted to you by sowing that seed on good soil (serving time productively), and in due season you will reap a bountiful harvest. That is the blessing of the biblical principle of sowing and reaping. *"A man reaps what he sows"* (Galatians 6:7).

LIBRARY

What better place besides the chapel is there for some quiet time in a correctional facility? I can't think of one. I was a law clerk for seven years at the last facility I was housed at, and I can honestly say that the time I spent at the library on the days I worked was some of the most productive, peaceful, and quiet time I had during those last several years of my incarceration.

> *"The library was the place where I penned all of my writing projects and where God revealed to me His purpose for my life regarding ministry and business."*

The library was the place where I penned all of my writing projects and where God revealed to me His purpose for my life regarding ministry and business. It is where I drafted most of my creative ideas. It was my own personal sanctuary away from all the drama that occurred elsewhere in the prison on any given day, and it can be yours too.

If you enjoy reading or writing, then the library is the place to invest time doing so. I encourage you to spend time reading when you are at the library, even if it is only a few pages of a book, and sharpening your writing skill if you desire to write. Reading and writing are good ways to improve your communication skills and are a valuable investment of time. It was one of the most valuable investments of time I made during my incarceration; one that has definitely paid off. The book you are reading is proof of that.

If you are appealing your conviction or pursuing some other legal remedy, the law library, which practically every jail and prison in America has, is the best place to do so. Whatever situation case-wise you currently find yourself in, be it a misdemeanor or a felony conviction, if you are trying to get your conviction overturned on appeal or seeking some other form of post-conviction relief, you are going to have to invest some quality time researching the law and how it applies to your case. Your freedom may depend on it.

It does not matter if you are fortunate enough to have an attorney handling your case, because no one knows your case better than you do. The time you invest familiarizing yourself with the law and how exactly it applies to your case, even the minutest details, will be time well-invested. After all, it is YOUR case. You alone have to decide how important your freedom is to you. The answer to that question is what motivates inmates who are serious about their freedom to invest time during their incarceration familiarizing themselves with the law. It is what motivated me. It is what should motivate you.

Although I was fortunate to have an attorney represent me at trial and on my appeals, all of which I lost, I did not allow that to deter me from investing time learning the law and how it applied to my case. Even though I did not win any of my appeals, the time I invested learning the law, not only as it applied to my case, but in general, and teaching other inmates what I knew about the law, and assisting those who were not fortunate enough to have an attorney representing them, was very satisfying to me. This too was a valuable investment of time. Any time you invest time helping another human being, you are managing time productively, this includes another inmate.

If you are a law clerk or have knowledge of the law, you too can serve time productively by investing time teaching other inmates what you know about the law, or assisting them with their cases, particularly those who are indigent and in dire need of legal assistance. Not only will you be serving time productively, you will be doing a good deed as well. In God's eyes, that is huge and He will reward you accordingly (Proverbs 11:25b; Matthew 25:40)

Anything you do during your incarceration to feed your mind with positive things will keep it from becoming idle. If you keep your mind from becoming idle, the devil will not be able to make it his playground. Remember: *a mind is a precious thing to waste.* Serve your time productively and you will not waste yours.

> **"Do not conform to the pattern of this world any longer, but be transformed by the renewing of your mind. Then you will be able to test and approve what God's will is—his good, pleasing and perfect will" Romans 12:2**

THOUGHT PROVOKERS
Chapter Two: Soul Time

1. When you invest time feeding your mind with productive thoughts, you are less prone to engage in unproductive activities. What do you consistently feed your mind with? _____
   _____
   _____
   _____

2. If a man does not work, then neither shall he _____.

3. If academic and vocational programs are offered at the facility you are housed at, how much time have you/do you/will you invest(ed) pursuing either of these during your incarceration? _____
   _____
   _____
   _____

4. If you invest a portion of your day in school or on a work-related assignment while incarcerated, how will that benefit you when you are released?_____
   _____

5. Work becomes an act of worship to God when you invest time doing it with a cheerful attitude. What is your attitude towards work? _____
   _____
   _____

Every inmate has a gift, talent, skill that he/she can invest time cultivating. Discover your's and cultivate it.

-Three-
BODY TIME

"Do you not know that your bodies are temples of the Holy Spirit, who is in you, whom you have received from God?" - 1 Corinthians 6:19

HEALTH

How important is your health to you? My hope is that it is very important to you during your incarceration. If you were not serious about your health prior to your incarceration, now is a good time to get serious. What time is it? It's body time!

Managing body time is just as important as managing spirit time, soul time, money time, and social time. If you are suffering from a physical ailment that threatens to cut your life short, investing time in your health is imperative. Whatever the ailment might be, it can be kept in check longer than you think by praying and believing you receive your healing according to the Word of God, and by exercising, eating right, and getting enough sleep each day.

You can preserve your health while incarcerated if you do your part. What is your part? To manage wisely the time you have by exercising, eating properly, drinking enough water, getting enough rest each day, and eliminating bad habits like tobacco, alcohol, drugs and anything else that shortens your life span.

Prior to my incarceration, I was not managing my health. I never gave it much thought. I was too naïve to realize how much damage I was doing to my body by using drugs, drinking alcohol, and smoking cigarettes. I began using these "body killers" (as I call them) at the age of twelve.

It was not until I went to prison that I chose to start managing my health. That was during my first year of incarceration. I was twenty years old. I used to go to the yard and the gym and see inmates weight lifting, doing aerobics, and playing different types of sports. It was then that I chose to start taking care of my "temple" (body).

Not a moment to waste, though I wasted precious moments in many other ways, I hooked up with this brother who was housed in the same unit that I was. Mr. Physique, as I dubbed him, looked like a professional bodybuilder. The guy was built! He had 2.9 percent body fat and massive muscle mass and definition, two key components if you desire to have that kind of physique, which I did not. I just wanted to have a nice physique.

Just because a person looks healthy does not necessarily mean they are.

I am not saying you have to have a Mr. Physique style physique to be healthy. Just because a person looks healthy does not necessarily mean they are. But you need to have some measure of mass and definition to have a decent looking physique. The two go hand in hand.

I started working out with Mr. Physique soon after we met. He took me on as his bodybuilding project and began teaching me various weight-training routines and calisthenics exercises for the different muscle groups, and how each exercise is vital for building muscle mass and definition. This was in January 1985. By September of that year, I had already gained twenty-five-pounds, most of it muscle mass, and my physique was starting to show signs of definition. More importantly,

I felt better physically than I ever had. Although I was weight lifting and doing calisthenics twice a day, five days a week, the benefit to me was not just physical. I was also managing time despite not having any real perception of time management at the time.

I enjoyed working out so much that it became a lifestyle to me, one that I maintained for the duration of my incarceration; and it did not stop after my release. I am still working out consistently to this day. It is truly a lifestyle for me, and my health has benefitted as a result. Had I not taken my health seriously during my incarceration by investing time at being disciplined with my workouts, participating in cardio-enhancing sports, watching my diet, drinking proper amounts of water, and getting the right amount of sleep each day, I would look and feel many years older than I actually am.

Instead, I look and feel many years younger than I actually am. This is precisely why I continue to follow the tips I am sharing with you in this chapter. Each of these tips is a daily priority in my management of time. If you are serious about your health, they should be yours as well. If you are not serious about your health at this time, then I encourage you to get serious. It could mean the difference between being unhealthy and remaining that way, or getting healthy and staying that way. Not only will you benefit physically by taking care of your health, you will be serving time productively in the process.

WEIGHT TRAINING
Any bodily exercise that enhances or maintains physical fitness and overall health and wellness is imperative during a period of incarceration. Weight training is no exception. It is one of the best ways to get healthy and stay healthy during your incarceration. It is also a valuable way to manage time. But just as with anything else you do during your incarceration that is beneficial to your overall growth and well-being, weight training takes time, discipline, and consistency to achieve a desired result. Anything short of this and all you will be doing is going through the motions, not seeing any gains.

If you are not willing to invest the time to be disciplined and consistent in the other key areas of your life (spirit, soul, money, social), you might find it difficult to do so where your weight training is concerned. There are no shortcuts in this area of exercise. It is imperative that you take weight training seriously in order to benefit from it and avoid getting injured.

I lost count of how many inmates approached me during my incarceration asking if they could work out with me. They knew I was serious because they saw me in the gym a minimum of five-days a week, and because I had the type of physique that proved my routines worked. Since I was disciplined and consistent, I was able to invest the time and achieve the desired result. A man reaps what he sows (Galatians 6:8). I reaped exactly what I sowed with weight training, and you can too, if you are disciplined and consistent with it.

If you are currently weight training and have been for some time, and are satisfied with the results, then you are reaping what you sow. Consider your time in the gym as time well-managed. Doing this will make the time you invest weight training more meaningful and your goals more attainable. For those of you who are not currently weight training, or have never weight trained, I encourage you to try it. If you do, try to set aside a minimum of three-days a week to weight train in the gym or on the yard, whichever is convenient for you.

"Do not believe the myth that doing ten sets of an exercise (any exercise) involving weights, or even calisthenics exercises, will shock your muscles and cause them to grow faster and bigger and make you stronger."

When you weight train it is important to work each body part (chest, back, shoulders, arms, legs, and abdominals) at least once a week, preferably twice a week. Do a minimum of three exercises per body part, three sets per exercise, eight to twelve repetitions (reps) per set. Always remember to stretch before and after each workout and do a warm-up set of each exercise of the body part you are working on prior to doing your regular sets.

Do not believe the myth that doing ten sets of an exercise (any exercise) involving weights, or even calisthenics exercises, will shock your muscles and cause them to grow faster and bigger and make you stronger. It will not. If anything, you will be tearing your muscles down instead of building them up. You may eventually injure yourself, which you certainly do not want to do. Weight training injuries can wreak havoc on your body. I once injured my lower back doing dead-lifts and the recovery time set me back a few months.

If you do not have any motivation to weight train and need a healthy dose, hook up with an experienced weight lifter at your facility that knows what he is doing and won't mind taking you on as a bodybuilding project. How will you know who to pick? Look for someone who invests a considerable amount of time weight lifting in the gym or on the yard. That is a person who is serious about his health. That is the kind of person you want to weight train with; someone who can help you reach your weight lifting goals.

Ask that person if you can be his workout partner. If he agrees, pay close attention to what he instructs you to do. Ask him to write you a copy of his workout routine and try to memorize each exercise (i.e., what it is called, which muscle group(s) it targets, and which weights are used, barbells, dumbbells, Universal machine, etc.).

If by chance you cannot find someone suitable to be your workout partner, do not let that discourage you. Go to the gym and spend some time observing how other inmates workout (i.e., what muscle group they are working, what exercises they are doing, and what type of weights they are using). Or you can always go to the library and look at fitness magazines like *Muscle Fitness* or *Men's Health*. These magazines contain a lot of valuable information that can help you decide which workout routine fits you best.

Once you have a workout routine you like, your next step is to put it into effect. Set up a workout schedule of at least three days a week, making sure it does not keep you from staying focused on other equally important activities during your incarceration. Learn to multitask and you will discover that managing spirit time, soul time, body time, money time, and social time will become second nature to you.

Getting in shape and staying in shape requires a serious investment of time, so do not try to become Mr. or Mrs. Muscle overnight. Your goal should not just be to get "buff," but to get healthy, if you are not already there, and to stay healthy.

Weight training is serious business. If you decide to make it part of your exercise regimen, approach weight training seriously so that you can avoid injuries and get the maximum benefit. Once you get yourself established, you will be managing that portion of your day, on your workout days, productively.

CALISTHENICS, CARDIO, AND CHIROPRACTIC:
Calisthenics & Cardio
A strong cardiovascular and central nerve system is something every athlete must have to compete at a certain level. For the inmate who is at the beginner, intermediate, or advanced level of exercising, be it weight training or any other type of sport, having a strong cardiovascular and central nerve system is just as important. Maintaining a consistent calisthenics, cardio and chiropractic exercise routine is a good way to keep your cardiovascular and central nerve system strong. It is an excellent warm up prior to exercising (weight lifting, other sports), and just as beneficial post-exercise.

During my incarceration, I always did calisthenics and cardio exercises before and after each workout even though my workout routines were physically taxing. You can choose whether to do calisthenics and cardio exercises before or after your workouts (or before and after), or on a separate day altogether, whichever works best for you.

> *"Maintaining a consistent calisthenics, cardio, and chiropractic exercise routine is a good way to keep your cardiovascular and central nervous system strong."*

One of the reasons I did calisthenics before each workout, and cardio exercises after each workout, was because of time constraints. I found that doing calisthenics before I hit the weights not only gave me an added boost of energy, but I was able to maximize my time at the gym doing my workout routine. I invested time just after breakfast, while waiting in my cell for the gym line to be called, to do pre-workout calisthenics. The pre-workout calisthenics I did then (and still do now) include jumping jacks, push-ups, and deep-knee bends (three sets of 25-50 reps per exercise). After each workout, I did cardio by jogging at a moderate pace for ten minutes, and then at a fast pace for another ten minutes. I also did the above calisthenics exercises in my cell whenever the facility I was housed at went on lockdown. Calisthenics and cardio exercises do justice for the cardiovascular system and help burn body fat. That is why I still do them.

Aerobics, treadmill, stationery bike, and elliptical all serve their purpose. If you can incorporate one or all of them in your workout routine, I encourage you to do so. They too work wonders for the cardiovascular system. At the end of the day, you have the choice to follow my routine or develop one of your own that you feel comfortable with. Whichever calisthenics and cardio routine you develop, give it your all. Your cardiovascular system will reward you for it.

A word of caution: whatever you do, do not become obsessed with it.

Your body needs rest (which we will discuss later in this chapter). I recommend no more than five days a week of calisthenics and cardio exercises; however you can fit that into your schedule. I now work out Monday, Tuesday, Thursday and Friday, and rest on Wednesday, Saturday and Sunday in order to give my body enough recovery time between workouts. At my age, rest is a must do!

Whichever calisthenics and cardio exercise routine you decide to do, if you are disciplined and consistent, you will get the maximum results from it. I stayed disciplined and consistent with physical exercise throughout my entire incarceration. I continue to be disciplined and consistent in my management of the time I invest in my physical health. My body thanks me for it every day, and yours will too. The time you invest in your health through weight training, calisthenics, and cardio is time served productively. Let that be your motivation.

Chiropractic

With respect to chiropractic, this is imperative for EVERYONE to incorporate in their body time. Our central nerve system is the body's "operations center." All of the body's functions begin here. If you have *subluxation* (a symptom of the spinal column, i.e. misalignment of one or more areas in your spinal cord), which actively alters neurological functions (central nerve system), you will eventually experience health problems directly related to the area of subluxation. A chiropractic adjustment of the problem area will begin to correct it almost immediately. This in turn allows the nerve/body organ it is connected to, to heal itself. When your spinal column is healthy, your body functions the way it was designed to.

But, when your spinal column is misaligned, the life-giving power of your nerve system is interrupted. This is subluxation, and it will cause painful symptoms and illnesses to occur. At this point, you will need to see a chiropractor and begin getting adjustments. Failure to do so will result in deterioration of your health in some measure. Whenever you see an elderly person walking "hunch-back", that is a sign of spinal deterioration as a result of neglect. Unless you want to end up that way in your latter years, I advise you to see a chiropractor (if you're able to) as soon as you are released.

I began seeing a chiropractor as soon as I completed my parole term. I first had to let my wife bend my arm a bit before I agreed to give chiropractic care a chance. I can say that it has improved my overall health significantly. I once had acid reflux and lower back pain, both in very annoying measure. The acid reflux is down to a bare minimum, and the lower back pain (especially when I get out of bed in the morning) is nonexistent. My energy level is way up, I have normal and consistent bowel movements daily (I know, TMI), I eat healthier, and I sleep like a baby EVERY night!

> *"Everyone has some measure of subluxation. Those who catch it early enough are able to get it corrected with chiropractic care."*

Everyone has some measure of subluxation. Those who catch it early enough are able to get it corrected with chiropractic care. The majority who don't end up with permanent damage to their spine and a host of health issues as they age. The upside of catching subluxation early is that your body can begin to heal naturally, the way it was intended to, from even the most common things such as colds, flu, digestive issues, migraine headaches, etc. No more need to take medication for any of those things. Chiropractic care takes care of all that!

Granted, although you don't have access to chiropractic care in prison, if you're able to get this care once you're released, then you should. I highly recommend it! You can go on line and obtain information about all the chiropractors in the community you plan to reside in.

SPORTS AND LEISURE TIME ACTIVITIES
Another excellent way to serve time productively and stay healthy

during your incarceration is to engage in as many sports and other leisure time activities as possible. I love all sports and participated in sports and leisure time activities as much as I could during my incarceration. These activities were a productive way for me to serve time because they were good for my health and they were a lot of fun. They also kept me proactive on the other productive activities I mention throughout this book.

Although I was not able to engage in sports and other leisure time activities while on parole (I was on electronic home monitoring during my entire parole term), once I completed my parole term I began to play sports and engage in leisure time activities again for the same reasons I did during my incarceration: they're a lot of fun, they're good for my health, and they keep me proactive on other productive activities. "AS A MAN THINKS, SO IS HE" (Proverbs 23:7).

When you play sports, you use many of your muscles and burn fat. The latter is a plus if you're trying to lose weight. I personally compare playing sports to doing cardio because the health benefits to your body and your overall health are one and the same: *awesome!* You already know this if you play sports. If you don't, then test my theory for yourself. You will be amazed at the results.

Whether you have never played sports or do not play them very well is not important. What is important is that you play, period! You do not have to be a pro athlete to play any sport. If you are serious about maintaining good health and desire to serve time productively during your incarceration, then I suggest you set aside a minimum of three days a week to play sports, more if you can fit that much leisure time into your schedule without taking away from other productive activities you might be involved in. Never sacrifice one productive activity for another. Learn to multitask and you will become a more efficient manager of your time.

There are various leisure time activities other than sports that you can engage in, such as billiards, Ping-Pong, foosball, bocce ball, chess, checkers, bingo, cards, Uno, Scrabble, Monopoly, arts & crafts, and so on. All of these leisure time activities can easily fall under the banner of *serving time productively,* if you engage in them on a leisure time basis and do not allow any of them to become the only thing that you do.

Remember, the whole purpose of serving time productively is to always be mindful of the time you invest doing daily activities in any of the five areas this book covers. That includes topics I may not have covered in each of these five areas that you may want to incorporate yourself. This stuff works! Anytime you invest time engaged in productive activities, you are managing time wisely.

DIETING:
Food
How much time do you spend eating or even thinking of food? Establishing and managing timely, disciplined, consistent, and regulated healthy dieting patterns and eating times can be difficult for some inmates, simply because of the environment they are confined to. It took years for me to discipline myself to diet right on a consistent basis during my incarceration, because I love food and had access to lots of it, even when I was not working the kitchen detail. Unless you are a vegetarian or already have a consistently healthy diet, I am certain that dieting properly is not easy for you either.

Inmates do not have the luxury of "menu variety." The inmate commissary does not exactly offer a variety of wholesome foods either, which makes it more difficult to maintain a healthy and balanced diet. That does not mean you cannot or should not try to diet properly during your incarceration. Nor does it mean you cannot manage time in this important area of your life. The truth is you can and you should.

If we are what we eat, then dieting should be done in a timely,

> *"If we are what we eat, then dieting should be done in a timely, disciplined, consistent, and regulated manner."*

disciplined, consistent, and regulated manner. Not every other day or when you are feeling it, but daily. Do not make the excuse that you cannot diet properly because you are incarcerated. You and I both know that you can. If you truly care about your physical well-being, you will take your diet seriously by eating healthy as often as you can.

Having served as much as time I did, I will be the first to admit that prison food is not something to write home about. It is under cooked, overcooked or just flat-out not edible. This, however, should not be an excuse for not eating it. Everyone has to eat. Trying to keep your body fed with food items you can purchase on the commissary is not going to cut it, particularly for the long-term. You probably already know this but haven't taken steps to address it. I tried living off commissary food for months at a time at one of the facilities I was housed at. After about the third month I began to wonder why I was feeling sluggish and not able to think clearly when working on one of my writing projects.

There were plenty of times I had to pass on certain meals simply because I could not eat what was being served. So I would eat whatever vegetable(s) was on the menu and a salad, if one was available, along with whatever fruit(s) was being served, if any. My point is if vegetables and fruits were the only food items I could eat on certain days, then I made sure to eat them. You should too, on those days when you cannot stomach a certain meal. Momma said there'd be days like this, didn't she? It's sad that those of us who have served time had to discover how true that saying is, in prison of all places!

Don't get me wrong. I am not saying not to eat the food items sold on the commissary. Just do not make them your entire diet. There are several "somewhat healthy" food items you can and should eat whenever possible: tuna, sardines, mackerel, fish steaks, chunk white chicken, beans, rice, oatmeal, mixed nuts, pretzels, and honey, to name a few. You can eat any of these food items in moderation and not have to worry about wrecking yourself nutritionally. Moderation is the operative word. Stay mindful about the kind and amount of all the food you eat.

Whatever you do, try your best to avoid junk food as much as possible. There is nothing nutritionally hazardous about indulging on a snack every now and then, meaning once or twice a week at most, and only if you exercise regularly. It makes zero sense to exercise, especially if your goal is to lose weight, if you are going to splurge on junk food daily and negate all the hard work you do in the gym. Why even bother!

If you manage the time you spend dieting and watch what you eat, your body will reward you. What you eat is just as important as when you eat and how much you eat. If dieting properly is not important to you, then eating junk food will be of no consequence to you. I hope, for your sake, that you are not of that mindset either during or after your incarceration.

> *"Although many take it for granted, water is essential to the overall health of the human body. We simply cannot survive without it"*

Water

The consumption of this life-sustaining element is just as important as eating the right foods. Although many take it for granted, water is essential to the overall health of the human body. We simply cannot survive without it. That is why the Earth is surrounded by it. If you exercise regularly, as we all should, drinking water is imperative. It helps to maintain proper muscle tone by giving muscles their natural ability to contract and prevents dehydration. It also helps to prevent sagging skin that usually follows weight loss. Shrinking cells are buoyed by water, which plumps the skin and leaves it clear, healthy, and resilient.

I am certain you know how easy and often you can get constipated in prison if your diet is unbalanced and you are not getting the proper amount of fiber. Water can relieve that. A lack of water will exacerbate it. When the body does not get enough water, it siphons what it needs from internal sources. The colon is a primary source. What is the result? Constipation! However, when you drink enough water each day, normal bowel function usually returns. Constipation can lead to sour stomach and can cause more serious health problems, too. You can avoid that simply by drinking enough water.

Water, incredible as it may seem, is quite possibly the single most important catalyst in losing weight and keeping it off. A decrease in water intake will cause fat deposits to increase, while an increase in water intake can actually reduce fat deposits.

Plus-size people have larger metabolic loads. Since water is the key to fat metabolism, it follows that the plus-size person needs more water, and regular exercise to go with it. If you are a plus-size person and are not happy being that size, I recommend you put together a time-efficient schedule for exercise, dieting, and water intake. No matter how plus-size you are, you will be on your way to getting where you want and need to be physically.

For those of you with water retention issues, excess salt (sodium) may be to blame. The body will tolerate sodium in certain amounts. The more sodium you consume, the more water your system retains to dilute it. Getting rid of unneeded sodium is easy, just drink more water! As it is forced through your kidneys, it flushes away excess sodium. That is a good thing. Too much sodium can cause high blood pressure, which can lead to other serious health issues like diabetes and heart disease.

So how much water intake, exactly, is enough? It can vary from person to person. But on average, you should drink a minimum sixty ounces (three, twenty-ounce bottles or approximately two quarts) daily. If you are plus-size, you will need one additional eight-ounce glass for every twenty-five pounds of excess weight. If you do not know how much you are supposed to weigh for a person of your height, sign-up for sick-call and ask your facility's doctor or one of the nurses. They should be able to tell you exactly how much you should weigh, according to your height and build. You may also want to get your body mass index (BMI) checked. For males it should be between 16-25 percent; for females, 23-30 percent. Anything higher for either male or female in their respective ranges can be unhealthy.

You should also increase your water intake if you exercise regularly, or if the weather is hot and humid. If bottled water is sold at your facility's commissary, I recommend you keep them stocked if you can. If you choose to do this but cannot afford to purchase multiple bottles, or are only allowed to buy a certain amount of bottles each time you shop, then buy what you can and reuse the bottle(s). You should sanitize the bottle(s) you drink from with warm water at least twice a day to kill germs and bacteria that can quickly build up inside the bottle and on the spout. Make sure to discard the bottle after three days' use.

To effectively manage your *amount* of water intake and the *time* of your water intake, try using the following schedule: one 16.9 oz. bottle every three hours. If your goal is to lose weight, drink another 16.9 oz. bottle between 8 P.M. and 9 P.M. Do not worry about having to get up in the middle of the night to use the bathroom; the benefit to your body is worth the annoyance when you see the pounds start to come off. If you follow these simple and practical tips in the daily management of time regarding your water intake, you will be managing body time wisely.

REST

Solomon, who, second only to Jesus, was the wisest human ever to walk the face of the Earth, wrote: *"There is a time for everything, and a season for every activity under heaven"* (Ecclesiastes 3:1). Managing time is applicable in everything we do. Rest is no exception. We should work when it is time to work, play when it is time to play, and rest when it is time to rest.

> *"We should work when it is time to work, play when it is time to play, and rest when it is time to rest."*

Depriving ourselves of enough rest is a sure way to "crash and burn" (wear ourselves out). That makes it unhealthy, to say the least. Even Jesus, the Creator of the Universe (John 1:3; Colossians 1:16) knew when to rest. He rested after creating the heavens, the earth, and man and woman (Genesis 2:1-2), and then instituted a day of rest called the Sabbath (Genesis 2:3), which He commands us to observe, just as He did (Exodus 20:8-11; Hebrews 4:1-11). He did all of this *before* He stepped off His throne in Heaven and came to Earth, before He ever created man, because, in His infinite wisdom, He foreknew that we, as fallible human beings, would need rest in our otherwise hectic lives.

When Jesus (the God-man) walked among us, He regularly went off to a solitary place not only to pray, but to rest. Why would an omnipotent God need to rest? Because when He stepped out of eternity and took on the form of a human (Luke 1:28-31; 2:6-11; Colossians 2:5-11), His body, like ours, was subject to fatigue. Therefore, when He became tired and needed to rest, He rested.

Our Creator was wise enough to work when He was supposed to work, play when He wanted to play, and rest when He needed to rest. Jesus is the perfect example for us to follow because He created rest. And since He rested from His own work, then we, as His creation should rest from ours as well.

Just how much rest the human body needs has always been a point of debate. The medical and physical fitness communities stress that the human body needs at least eight hours of rest each day, particularly if you are on your feet for the other sixteen. When you are well-rested you are typically at your best. When you are not well-rested you may feel tired, sluggish, and cranky. I know I have.

Rest in the correctional setting is just as important to your overall physical health as it will be when you are released, perhaps even more so. If you are always on the go, it is imperative that you have a daily, regularly scheduled time to rest, be it at night or during the day, whichever is more suitable for you. The important thing is that you get enough rest each day. You can work, go to school, exercise, play sports, or burn the midnight oil each day and get by on a few hours of sleep. But eventually your brain will shut itself down, and when that happens, your body will shut itself down. You can avoid that. Just get enough rest.

If you are an early morning riser (5:00 am or earlier), then going to bed late (10:00 p.m. or after) can be counterproductive. If you are a night owl, then staying up all day without getting any rest is just as counterproductive. Whatever your schedule is, fitting rest into your daily management of time is essential to avoid crash and burn. However, do not end up sleeping your time away; that would be a gross mismanagement of time and you will not benefit from it any way. If anything, it will wreck your health, and eventually your life! (Proverbs 6:6-11).

If you cannot get at least eight hours of sleep each day, then try to supplement your rest time with daily naps. You will be surprised at how much a nap will reenergize you, even if it is only a fifteen-minute nap. During my incarceration, I used to take a nap every day from 3-4 P.M. (count time). I did that the entire twenty-four years I served (give or take a few days). I even took naps during lockdowns because to me being locked in a cell was not much different from being out of it.

Either way I was still incarcerated.

At the end of the day, I did not allow much of anything to interfere with my rest or nap time. I napped at the same time every day, and slept at the same time every night. Managing wisely my rest and nap time each day enabled me to be at my best at everything I did, which was a plus for me being that I was one of those guys who was always on the go. I may have been incarcerated, but I took full advantage of the movement I was blessed to have within the confines of each facility I was housed at.

> *"If you are serious about managing body time by taking care of your health, you must be committed to getting enough rest each day"*

If you are serious about managing body time by taking care of your health, you must be committed to getting enough rest each day. And, you must set aside time to take naps every day. You will begin to notice a considerable increase in your energy level and this will enable you to be more productive with your time each day. That's managing time!

BODY KILLERS

Drugs, liquor, pills, cigarettes, I call these body killers because that is exactly what they are. If you use any or all of them, you are slowly but surely killing yourself. As hard as it is to get good health care in prison, why would you subject yourself to that?

There was a time during my incarceration when health care was readily available and free of charge. However, when people in society began complaining about inmates getting free health care, when they themselves could not afford it, the Department of Corrections decided to start charging a co-pay of $2.00 just to see a nurse. So what quality of health care am I referring to? Well, if you're fortunate, you might get some Motrin to alleviate whatever medical condition you're dealing with. Sad, isn't it? That is one of the reasons I chose to confess my healing in Christ (Isaiah 53:5) whenever the Enemy attempted to attack me with some sickness or injury, instead of subjecting myself to the frustrating process an inmate has to endure just to see a doctor.

While there are people who use body killers for years, even decades, without suffering serious or fatal health effects, why play Russian Roulette with your life and take for granted however much time you have on this Earth by trying to be one of them? That's suicide!

If you are currently using a body killer(s), you are already committing suicide, albeit on your body's timetable. Your body will know when it has had enough. When that time comes, and it will, there will not be much of anything you will be able to do to reverse the damage. By then it might be too late! When I think of the damage I could have done to my body because of the body killers I used, I remind myself of the lesson I learned from it: INVEST TIME IN YOUR OVERALL HEALTH AND TAKE YOUR BODY SERIOUSLY!

It's because of God's mercy I was fortunate to have walked away from using body killers without suffering any health effects. It is as if I had never used them. Now I'm making up for all the time I mismanaged abusing my body and I'm enjoying the benefits of living a healthy lifestyle. You can, too, if you use body killers. Do not wait until it's too late. By then, you may not have any lifestyle left to enjoy!

When you invest time during your incarceration taking care of your health, you are serving time productively. If you are currently mismanaging time by neglecting your health, especially if you're using body killers, then I encourage you to be wise and get busy managing time in this important area of life. *"...Don't you know that your body is the temple of the Holy Spirit, who lives in you? You are not your own. You were bought at a price. Therefore, honor God with your body"* (1 Corinthians 6:19-20). What more can I say? This verse of Scripture sums up this entire chapter.

THOUGHT PROVOKERS
Chapter Three: Body Time

1. Just because a person looks healthy does not necessarily mean they are. Have you/do you/will you invest(ed) on your overall health?

   _____

   _____

2. You should set aside a minimum of (3) days a week to exercise. True or False_____

3. Maintaining a consistent calisthenics, cardio and chiropractic routine is a proven way to keep your cardiovascular and central nervous system strong. Since you are not able to get chiropractic care in prison, do you incorporate calisthenics and cardio in your exercise routine? _____

   _____

4. When you manage what you eat, how much you eat, and when you eat, you are serving time productively. Have you/do you/will you invest(ed) time doing any of the above?_____

   _____

5. Sublaxation is the misalingment of your spinal cord. Everyone has some measure of it throughout the course of their life. Chiropractic care can heal a person of this if caught early enough. True or False_____

   When you invest time during your incarceration taking care of your health, you serve time productively. If you invest body time wisely while you're incarcerated, you will be encouraged and equipped to continue doing it when you're released. Invest body time daily.

Four

MONEY TIME

"The blessing of the Lord brings wealth, and he adds no trouble to it" - **Proverbs 10:22**

God has a lot to say about money. After all, He created it. There are over 2,350 verses of Scripture in the Bible that speak on everything we need to know about managing money. The Word of God is mankind's go-to guide for managing money. If you want to learn how to manage money, study the Bible. There isn't a better book on the subject.

Since God created money and is the universal expert on the subject, we should heed what He has to say about it. He implicitly mentions the topic of money repeatedly throughout His Word because He wants us to know His perspective on this important area of life. If managing time is important to you, then managing money should be just as important, because time is money.

You can serve time productively during your incarceration by maximizing the time you invest learning how to manage money. And when you are released, you should not have any problem managing this important area of life; you will already know how to be disciplined at managing, tithing, giving, saving, budgeting, investing, and spending.

Everything you do during your incarceration is a reflection of what you will be doing when you are released. Managing or mismanaging money is no exception. By investing time learning to manage money, you can avoid the pitfalls that come with not knowing what to do with money once you have it.

More importantly, to be successful at managing money when you are released, it is imperative that you invest time regularly during your incarceration learning how to do this. Had I not invested time during my incarceration learning how to manage money, I would not be as disciplined in this area of life as I am today. A man reaps what he sows (Galatians 6:8). I sowed the time and reaped the knowledge.

MANAGE IT

If you are fortunate enough to be housed in a facility that pays inmates to work and you have a work detail, then you have money you can manage. But do not be fooled into thinking that you have to have money in order to learn how to manage it. It is simply not true. It does not hurt to have it, but you do not need it to learn how to manage it. What you need is discipline, patience and the desire to learn. To do this you have to be willing to invest the time, and since time is something you have, why not invest it wisely?

The amount of time you invest learning and applying this important skill during your incarceration, will determine how successful you will be at it when you are released. That means you should be investing as much time as you can learning as much as you can about managing money. The library is a good place to start. Invest time there reading books, magazines, journals, and anything else you can find relating to money. If you have access to a TV, watch financial news programs as often as possible. You will be surprised at how much you can learn (see Index for channels).

If you are enrolled in college at your facility or taking correspondence courses, be sure to take classes such as economics, business mathematics,

73

> *"One of the most important things to remember while you are learning to manage money is you will only get out of it what you put into it."*

finance, and accounting. One of the most important things to remember while you are learning to manage money is you will only get out of it what you put into it. That is a universal law that applies to everything we do in life and money is no exception.

If you are serious about becoming an astute manager of your finances, sow time learning how to become one and you will reap the harvest. The rest of this chapter deals with tithing, giving, saving, budgeting, investing, and spending; things that are vital to a person's financial health. If you care about your financial health, you will be wise to take heed.

TITHE IT

Everything we have comes from God, whether we believe that or not. So, when we refuse to sow into His Kingdom a portion of what He has given to us, so that He can use it through us as He desires, we rob Him. God does not *need* our money or any of our stuff. He simply wants us to use it for His glory, not ours. Do you selfishly keep all of what God blesses you with, or do you sow a portion into His Kingdom? Take some time, if necessary, to reflect on this. If you are not tithing, now is a good time to start.

The Bible makes the purpose of tithing very clear: to put God first in our lives. We should give Him the first and best of what we have. What we do with our money shows what we value most. Sowing a portion of our income, time, resources, talents, skills, or gifts to God *first* (first fruits; Proverbs 3:9) immediately focuses our attention on God.

Although tithing is an Old Testament command and there is no New Testament precedent that says we "have" to tithe, it is still an option, you either do or you don't. A tithe (tenth) of everything from the land, whether grain from the soil or fruit from the trees, belongs to the LORD; it is holy to the LORD (Leviticus 27:30). Obedience is the first step toward receiving God's abundance; tithing is an act of faith that follows. Would you rather have ninety percent that is blessed or one-hundred percent that is cursed?

There are missed blessings for those who choose not to tithe and abundant blessings for those who do (Malachi 3:9-10). Once I learned about tithing, I began giving God the first ten percent of my work detail earnings, or "state pay" as it is called in the Illinois prison system. My highest pay was $72.50 a month. I could have used the excuse that I was not required to tithe because I was incarcerated and really did not have any money to give God ten percent, but I did not use that excuse. Instead, I chose to honor God by giving Him above my tithe. I would give $10.00 instead of $7.25, $5.00 instead of $4.50 when my pay was $45.00, and when my state pay was reduced to $30, 20, and eventually $15.00 a month, I still gave $5.00. In doing so, God blessed me by making sure my needs were always met according to His riches in glory in Christ Jesus (Philippians 4:19).

I never wanted for anything in prison during those years I was tithing. It is when I did not tithe that I experienced lack. That was during an eight month period after I lost a bid for clemency. I was angry with God. Once I got over my anger and repented, I realized why I was lacking and began to tithe again. The blessings began to flow once again as well. I also gave offerings whenever I was able to and that blessing was always given back to me in full measure (Luke 6:38). Giving offerings is just as important to receiving God's abundance as tithing is. I will show you why in the following section.

"The time we invest giving to those less fortunate is an investment that has eternal dividends."

GIVE IT

This is something most inmates find difficult to do simply because they feel they have nothing to give or cannot give any of what they have, be it time, money or possessions. Yet, it is no less important to adhere to than any other section of this chapter or book. In fact, it is the *most* important if you desire to be blessed and see increase in your life. The time we invest giving to those less fortunate is an investment that has eternal dividends. It is also one of the most productive ways to serve time because it comes with a dual blessing: God blesses you, so that you can bless others. *"One man gives freely, yet gains even more; another withholds unduly, but comes to poverty"* (Proverbs 11:24).

If we are generous with what God blesses us with, He will bless us with even more. However, *"if a man shuts his ears to the poor, he too will cry out and not be answered"* (Proverbs 21:13). Furthermore, "a stingy man is eager to get rich and is unaware that poverty awaits him" (Proverbs 28:22). If we are stingy with what we have, our only hope is that whatever we have will last until we breathe our last, because poverty will always be one step behind us.

We should never avoid reaching out to someone in need or we may one day find ourselves in need. But when you give, make sure you have the proper attitude so that your gift is acceptable to God. He is more interested in the *attitude* you give with than the *amount* that you give (1 Corinthians 9:7). Give "cheerfully" and this will result in a blessing that flows to you, the giver.

"He who refreshes others will himself be refreshed" (Proverbs 11:25), for *"A gift opens the way for a giver and ushers him into the presence of the great"* (Proverbs 18:16). As you bless others, God blesses you. When we give, God gives us more so that we can give more. Giving helps us gain and maintain a proper perspective on all that we have. We come to realize, with gladness of heart, that what we have is not really ours to begin with; we are merely stewards of all the resources that God entrusts to our care, be it time, money, possessions, gifts, talents, skills, etc. Therefore, giving to others enables us to honor God in a tangible way.

What then do we gain by giving? Freedom from enslavement to our possessions, the joy of helping others and, most importantly, God's blessing. *"He who gives to the poor will lack nothing, but he who closes his eyes to them receives many curses"* (Proverbs 28:27). The time we spend giving to others is an indication of where we are spiritually.

What we give to others should be considered a *gift*, not a high-interest loan that will benefit us more than them. Do not give to someone expecting something in return. That is not a gift, it's a loan! The Author of selfless giving, Jesus Christ, said "Give and it shall be given to you. A good measure, pressed down, shaken together and running over will be poured into your lap. For with the measure you use, it will be measured to you" (Luke 6:38). The Apostle Paul quotes Jesus as saying "It is better to give than to receive" (Acts 20:35).

Giving is a natural response of a good-hearted person. Only our God and Savior, Jesus Christ, can put such a quality as giving in a person's heart. Your willingness to give is more important than the amount you give. When you invest time giving to those in need, they might just be in a position to help you someday should you ever find yourself in need. When you give you express God's love to those you are giving to. It reflects your devotion to Him. God gives to us so that we can give to others.

Do not use incarceration as an excuse to avoid giving. There are inmates right where you are who could use a helping hand, and it does not have to be materially or financially. Giving goes way beyond that. If God has enabled you to be a giver, than give what you purpose in your heart to give and it shall be given back to you in good measure.

> *"You can invest time using your gift, talent or skill to help someone during your incarceration."*

Just do not make that the sole purpose of your giving. Remember, it is better to give than to receive.

God has blessed each of us with a gift, talent or skill. You can invest time using your gift, talent or skill to help someone in need during your incarceration, be it your cellmate or some other inmate(s) at your facility. For instance, if you have knowledge of the law, you can assist other inmates with their cases (i.e., Post-Conviction, appeals, etc.) There is a huge need for that type of assistance in correctional facilities, particularly with inmates who do not have legal representation because they cannot afford it. If you are a law clerk working at the law library at your facility, you are in the best position to perform such a service. You just have to be willing to "give of your time." You can rest assured that it will be time well-invested, because time that is invested helping a fellow inmate with something this important (or anything of importance) is time served productively.

Here is another example of how one can give in a correctional setting. Let's say you have the ability to teach others. You can invest time using that gift by tutoring fellow inmates at your facility who lack basic reading, writing, or math skills. You might even be able to get assigned as a tutor in the education department at your facility and be paid for it. Or, if you have a vocational skill (i.e., carpentry, electrical, plumbing, HVAC, etc.) you might be able to get assigned to a work detail in the vocational department at your facility tutoring other inmates. In either case, you will be honoring God by helping others, and serving time productively in the process.

So, how do you decide how much to give when giving money? You should first decide who might benefit the most from your giving, be it a church, relief agency, or an individual. You should then give what you have purposed in your heart to give, not reluctantly or under compulsion, for God loves a cheerful giver (2 Corinthians 9:7).

God made us stewards of the money He blesses us with, so it is not *our* money, it is *His!* But He allows us to decide how much to give. That is an awesome responsibility, one that we should never take lightly. When we give it should be in proportion with what God has given us. *"We should give of what we have, for is the willingness is there, the gift is acceptable according to what one has, not according to what he does not have"* (2 Corinthians 8:12).

Let me reiterate that it's not the amount of your giving, but the attitude of your heart when you give. Do not give $1.00 when you can give $10.00, or don't spend one-hour tutoring or mentoring a fellow inmate when you can invest two-hours. As with anything else in life, you only get out of giving what you put into it, *"For with the measure you use it will be measured to you"* (Luke 6:38).

We should be responsible in our giving. This applies to those who still have time to serve as well as to those are soon to be released. Give generously, but not to the extent that those who depend on you for financial support, whoever that might be, have to go without having their basic needs met. If you are fortunate enough to provide financial support to someone during or after your incarceration, as many men and women who have served time in state and federal prisons across this country have done, then do not shy away from that responsibility. Whether you are incarcerated or have already been released, you touch the very heart of God when you bless others who depend on you.

The principles you apply in giving financially are universal and can be applied in all areas of giving. *"But just as you excel in everything—in faith, in speech, in knowledge, in complete earnestness and in your love for us—see that you also excel in this grace of giving"* (2 Corinthians 8:7). *"Remember this: Whoever sows sparingly will also reap sparingly, and whoever sows generously will also reap generously"* (2 Corinthians 9:6). That passage of Scripture is based on God's law of sowing and reaping. If you give (sow) a little that is exactly what you will get in return. On the other hand, if you give generously you will be blessed generously.

When you invest time giving, whatever you give will be given back to you as Luke 6:38 says. It is a promise made by God. And God does not lie (Hebrews 6:18). You do not have to take my word on that.

Take God's Word, the Bible, and see for yourself that what He says is true. I do it every day and I have yet to be disappointed. I know in my heart the Word of God will never disappoint me. I am careful to correctly divide the word of truth (2 Timothy 2:15).

Because you are incarcerated you may hesitate to give if you dwell on not having enough to meet your own needs, or if the benefit to giving is not worth it to you. Do not let a lack of faith and trust in God keep you from giving freely, joyfully and generously. If God thinks it is worth it, then so should you. Besides, if you *"seek first the kingdom of God and his righteousness, all that you have need of shall be given to you"* (Matthew 6:33). Do your part and give generously so that God can do His part and bless you abundantly.

SAVE IT

How do you define saving? I define it as foregoing expenditure "today" (the present) so that I will have something to spend "tomorrow" (the future). *"In the house of the wise are stores of choice food and oil, but a foolish man devours all he has"* (Proverbs 21:20). This proverb is about *saving* for the future. The Lord Jesus taught us the importance of exercising due diligence in saving money. It is up to us to invest time applying that priceless knowledge.

> *"...those who spend all they have are spending more than they can afford! A wise person saves money and has it readily available when he needs it."*

The desire to acquire materialistic things sometimes pushes people to spend every penny they have, but those who spend all they have are spending more than they can afford! A wise person saves money and has it readily available when he needs it. If you have never saved money before, now is a good time to start. If all you can save is $5.00 a month the entire time you are incarcerated, you will at least have something saved up when you are released. That's better than walking out of prison penniless. Of course, if you can save more, by all means do so. The more you save, the more you will have. Whatever you do, do not pin your expectations on the "gate money" that most Departments of Corrections give inmates when they are released, as a means of having a lil' somethin' to fall back on. Have a lil' somethin' of your own to walk out of prison with, even if it is only $50.00 or $100.00. You will be amazed at how much better you will feel knowing you have money in your pocket that you saved during your incarceration.

You can start investing time now building up your post-incarceration nest-egg by saving up a certain amount of your state pay. You may have to deny yourself certain things that you are used to buying when you shop at the commissary (I am referring to wants, not needs). As hard as that may be to do at first, it will come naturally and be less painful each month, once you realize the money you are saving is for your benefit.

You should also save some of the money you receive from the outside sources I mentioned earlier if you are fortunate enough to be receiving such assistance. Every dollar you save is another dollar you will have. If you are blessed to have a correctional industries work detail, you should be able to save even more money. Again, the more you save the more you will have when you are released. Let that be your motivation as you invest time saving money for your release.

I know this is easier said than done. I know because I failed to save more money during my incarceration and I paid for it when I was released. It was not because I did not have more money to save, but because I chose to live comfortably and not deny myself anything I could afford. Before I began managing money wisely, I lived for today and did not give much thought for tomorrow where money was concerned. I did that by allowing the lengthy sentence I was serving to lure me into that negative mindset. That was a costly mistake, one I advise you to avoid making during your incarceration. The cost to you may be more than you can afford. It was for me.

Not only is saving money during your incarceration the smart thing to do, it is imperative! If you have money, you are going to be tempted to spend it today without giving much thought to whether you will need it tomorrow. That is exactly what I did repeatedly prior to learning how to manage money. I failed to apply some of the financial principles I am sharing with you in this chapter. Do not make the mistake I made.

Manage wisely whatever money you have, particularly where saving is concerned. I could have easily walked out of prison with a substantial amount of savings in a bank account. Instead I walked out of prison with almost no money. If you have not experienced that yet, for your sake I hope you will never have to. Trust me when I say it is not a good feeling.

> *"Be wise and invest the time that is necessary saving up a post-incarceration nest-egg."*

Sure, I had a solid support system in place when I was released and was blessed in many ways, but that is not the point. I should not have had to rely solely on that, and neither should you, even if you have a support system in place waiting for you upon your release. I could have and should have had more money saved up in advance, and so should you, if you want to avoid having a financial shortfall. Be wise and invest the time that is necessary saving up a post-incarceration nest-egg. This way, when you are released, you will have a head start and will be better prepared financially to reintegrate into society and face whatever economic challenges that await you.

If you have not already done so, you should open a savings account with a bank or credit union if your finances allow. Even if you have a year left to serve and believe you will be able to serve that time at the prison you are currently housed at, you can open a savings account with a local bank situated near the prison. Upon your release, you can close the account and open another account at a bank in the area where you plan to reside.

One of the reasons it is wise to open a savings account while you are still incarcerated is because you will not have quick access to spending that money on stuff (such as commissary) as you would by keeping it in your inmate trust fund account. The purpose of having a savings account while you are still incarcerated is to *save* money, not spend it. Be wise, then, by spending only what you need to spend and by saving all that you can save. Invest time putting together a monthly budget that you can realistically stick to while still incarcerated. Having a budget will motivate you to be disciplined with money, particularly where savings are concerned. I will discuss that in the next section.

Remember there are two types of savings: near-term and long-term. Near-term savings should be readily available in the event of an emergency. Long-term savings should be used to fund needs and goals. Saving money will enable you to do what the next section of this chapter touches on, not only while you are incarcerated, but more importantly when you are released. A wise man saves for the future. A foolish man spends all he has. Be wise and avoid the latter.

"A budget is a plan for spending money, and having one enables you to maintain an attitude of control in spending what's needed to reach financial goals and objectives."

BUDGET IT
This is an area of managing money that I strongly encourage you to invest as much time on as possible during your incarceration if you want to have a handle on your finances upon your release.

So what exactly is a budget? A budget is a plan for spending money, and having one enables you to maintain an attitude of control in spending what's needed to reach financial goals and objectives. If you have debt, budgeting is the only way to get out of debt so that you can tithe, give, save, and invest the money God blesses you with while still taking care of your most basic needs. It may not seem rewarding at first, but once applied you will begin to notice that you will always have enough money at the end of each month, instead of having "too much month" left at the end of the money.

The important thing to stay mindful of is that a budget is useful only if it is applied. It should be a carefully crafted plan for managing the money God blesses you with. However, in order to craft a budget you must begin with your current financial status. You have to determine exactly how much money you earn and how much you spend.

It is crucial to keep a detailed record of every dollar you earn and spend for at least a month in order to get an accurate assessment so that you can complete an estimated budget. If your monthly earnings are not the same, you will have to make a guesstimate of your annual earnings and divide that by 12 to come up with a workable number for your monthly earnings. Do not be alarmed if you have monthly or yearly expenditures that exceed your earnings. Almost every budget begins that way.

In order to deal with the issue of spending more than you earn, it is imperative that you either increase your earnings or decrease your spending. Once you are able to do this, maintaining a monthly budget will become second nature. However, the thought of not budgeting will always be there. Delete that thought the moment it enters your mind. Determine never to mismanage money again.

Carefully and periodically review your budget to make sure it is working the way you crafted it to. If you invest the time and manage your budget properly, you will be able to save a lot of money that you might otherwise spend. If you apply these principles, budgeting will work for you just like it works for me. All you have to do is invest the time and money. Follow the tips I just gave you regarding budgeting (the same tips I currently use) and see for yourself how they work.

INVEST IT

This is another area of money management I wish I had invested more time learning and applying during my incarceration. But I did not, so I had to play catch up with this when I was released. Do not make the same mistake. Invest time during your incarceration making financial investments for the future. When you are released, you will be glad you did.

> *"One of the most important principles you need to learn and apply so that you can become a successful investor is to spend less than you earn..."*

One of the most important principles you need to learn and apply so that you can become a successful investor is to spend less than you earn, which I touched on in the previous section of this chapter. One way to do this is to save and invest over a substantial period of time, the difference between what you earn and what you spend.

If you are wondering what investments to make that will yield consistent and profitable returns, get the advice of an experienced money manager that you can trust to manage your investments during and after your incarceration. Do a Google search of all the money managers in your area when you are released and find out which is the right one for you. It is prudent to apply patience when investing. If you want to improve your chances of making successful investments and avoid risky ones, you will need to learn everything you can about the type of investment you are putting your money into.

No investment is without risk. It is prudent, therefore, to *"...give your portions to seven, yes to eight, for you do not know what disaster may come upon the land"* (Ecclesiastes 11:2). In other words, don't lay all your eggs in one basket. Before you invest time and money in any investment, carefully and prayerfully consider the cost (Luke 14:28). This will keep you from wasting time and money.

If you devote time during your incarceration learning how to manage money and apply what you learn by being disciplined in the way you tithe, give, save, budget, and invest, you will be serving time productively. More importantly, when you are released, you will be better prepared to manage time in this important area of your life.

SPEND IT

This is the shortest section in this book, but one of the most important, so please pay close attention. If you have a paying work detail, the first thing you need to learn is to be a disciplined and faithful steward (manager) in the way you *spend* money. Just because you may not have bills to pay (barring the state you are in is not taxing you via asset forfeiture, child support, etc.), you should not feel free to spend whatever money you have, be it pay from your work detail, money being sent to you from outside sources, family, or friends, or savings you might have in a bank account, as if tomorrow does not matter. Tomorrow *does* matter.

How you spend money today will determine if you will have any to spend tomorrow. If you spend all that you have, you're spending more than you can afford! *"He who ignores discipline comes to poverty and shame"* (Proverbs 13:18).

If we fail to be disciplined and faithful stewards with the way we spend money, we do so at our own peril. However, if we practice discipline, we become faithful stewards of the financial resources God entrusts us with. When we are faithful stewards, God is able to entrust us with more resources so that we can advance His Kingdom even more. I encourage you, therefore, to become a disciplined and faithful steward in the way you spend money. Your financial future may depend on it!

THOUGHT PROVOKERS
Chapter Four: Money Time

1. Managing money time is a valuable investment while incarcerated. How you manage money today will determine if you will have any money to manage tomorrow. How well do you manage money?

    _____

    _____

2. What do you gain by giving to others? Freedom from enslavement to your possessions, the joy of helping others and, most importantly, God's blessing! How much time have you/do you/will you invest(ed) giving of your gift, talents, skills, etc., to others? _____

    _____

3. A wise person invests time saving for the future. A foolish person wastes time by spending all he has! Are you the former or the latter? _____

4. A budget is a plan for spending money, and having one enables you to maintain an attitude of control. Have you/do you/will you budget(ed) money during your incarceration, so that when you're released you will be more inclined to maintain one?

    _____

5. One of the most important principles you need to learn and apply in order to become a successful investor is to "sit down and count the cost before you begin to build" an investment portfolio. Are you willing to commit the time to learn how to become a successful investor? _____

    Those who spend more than they earn are spending more than they can afford!

-Five-

SOCIAL TIME

"If it is possible, as far as it depends on you, live at peace with everyone." - **Romans 12:18**

Do you consider yourself a social person? If not, have you taken the time to ask yourself why? In order to manage spirit time, soul time, body time, and financial time, it is imperative that you are able to manage social time as well. If you desire to be socially responsible upon your release, it is important that you invest time while incarcerated learning how to be effective at it. Although prison might seem like a difficult place to learn and apply social skills, it can also be an easy place because of the different people (inmates, staff, outside volunteers) you come in contact with every day.

You can learn to become a social person simply by choosing to *"live at peace with everyone"*, even with inmates or staff whom you do not associate with or interact with. At the end of the day, this is always a good thing. One thing I learned quickly during my incarceration is that in the volatile world of prison, it is better to be at peace with those around you than at war. The same applies in society, something I began practicing immediately upon my release.

In order to be a socially responsible person during your incarceration, and after your release, it is imperative that you focus on the following:

(1) Reconcile strained relationships, (2) Build new relationships, (3) Establish relationships with community-based organizations that are dedicated to helping inmates during and after their incarceration, (4) Train yourself to become an effective communicator and listener, (5) Cultivate your social skills daily so that you can become an effective people person, (6) Do volunteer work during and after your incarceration, and (7) Join a self-help group(s).

If you focus on doing these things during your incarceration, you will be laying the foundation for becoming a socially responsible member of society upon your release. You will be better prepared to transition from inmate to free citizen again. Even if you are not being released anytime in the near future, or if you are a lifer, you will still be working toward becoming a socially responsible person right where you are for the remainder of your sentence. That too, is a good thing, for this is one of the core principles of managing time in a correctional setting.

RECONCILE STRAINED RELATIONSHIPS
Outside The Wall
"The end of a matter is better than its beginning" (Ecclesiastes 7:8). During my quarter century of incarceration I came in contact with other inmates who, prior to their incarceration, had burned a bridge or two with someone they had been close to, whether it was an immediate family member, relative, friend, or business acquaintance.

The lingering effect of their falling out with that person troubled them. Most expressed regret about the role they played in the matter. Although they tried to come across as hardcore, something that a lot of men and women in prison feel they have to portray, I was able to look beyond the bravado right into their soul and feel their pain at no longer having a relationship with the person they had fallen out with.

I was able to relate to what they felt because I was experiencing the same drama at the time. I too had burned a few bridges prior to my incarceration; not with any of my family members, but with others I was close to at one time. As much as I hated to admit that I was wrong for crossing them that is exactly what I did in order to right a wrong.

During the first few days after my arrest in June 1984, while being held without bond at the infamous Cook County Jail, I began to contact the people I had wronged to try to reconcile these strained relationships. I was stunned at how quickly some of them had written me off and forgotten that I even existed. Not only did they refuse to accept my collect calls, they went as far as to have their phones blocked from receiving collect calls. I could have called them on a three-way, but did not even bother. I never heard from any of those people again. To this day, decades later, I do not know what became of them and it hurts that our friendship ended on those terms.

As for those I did make contact with, some of them made it clear that they were not interested in hearing anything I had to say; as far as they were concerned I did them wrong when I was on the streets and nothing else needed to be said. Then there were those who forgave me, but did not go out of their way to keep in touch. Still others who forgave me and made the effort to keep in touch, if only for a few years, eventually disappeared from the radar screen too.

> **"It does not pay to burn bridges with anyone, be it family, relatives, friends or business acquaintances, because you never know if you will be able to reconcile with them."**

I did what I could to reconcile these strained relationships, but the damage had already been done and no amount of damage control on my part was able to change that. That is what can happen when you burn bridges. I prayed about the situation and left the outcome to God. Fortunately, I still had my family, relatives, and close friends whom I didn't burn bridges with and who stood by my side the entire time I was incarcerated. Those are bridges

I will make sure I never burn. In fact, I have since made it one of my priorities to avoid burning bridges with anyone, for I desire to *"live at peace with everyone"*.

It does not pay to burn bridges with anyone, be it family, relatives, friends or business acquaintances, because you never know if you will be able to reconcile with them. Some relationships can be strained so badly that reconciliation becomes almost impossible. Use my example of the relationships I strained as a reason to avoid this. I had to learn this the hard way, as I am certain that many who are reading this book have had to as well. At the end of the day it is not a good feeling. The lingering effects of having a strained relationship with someone can cause emotional and health issues, two things no one wants, especially in a correctional setting. Prison is not a place you want to be if you are disowned by someone you have burned in some way, especially a family member. It is one thing to be disowned by friends while incarcerated, but something entirely different to be disowned by family. Some of the guys I referred to earlier had burned bridges with their own family and I witnessed up close and personal the emotional affect it had on them. It is hard enough being incarcerated without adding the stress of a strained relationship with one's family. Some of these guys snapped and did some foolish things that placed them in a worse situation than the one they were already in.

Prison officials are human and may even empathize with an inmate's situation, particularly where it concerns his or her family. But at the end of the day, they still have a job to do, and do it they will if an inmate commits an infraction. Your responsibility as an inmate is to make sure you do not cross that line, regardless of the issue you might be facing. That too I had to learn the hard way, on more than one occasion, while dealing with personal issues, and that is why I am advising you to avoid making that mistake.

"He who brings trouble on his family will inherit only wind" (Proverbs 11:29). One of the greatest blessings God gives us is family. There is

no greater bond of love than family. Everyone else may disown you, but family is for life. Therefore, falling out with family, be it because of anger or a selfish desire for independence, is about the craziest thing a person can do. Once you sever that cord, you forfeit all that the family unit provides.

Keep in mind, however, that this is not limited to just family. If you have burned bridges with anyone on the outside prior to your incarceration or during your incarceration, and still have not made an attempt to reconcile with that person, I encourage you to think about the near-term and long-term consequences of allowing pride to keep you from doing so sooner than later. Later might be too late to mend fences. Now is the time to reach out to that person, because you have time to do so.

I never put off for tomorrow what I can do today because tomorrow is not promised to anyone. Moreover, "...*today has enough trouble of its own*" (Matthew 6:34). If we defer something as important as being reconciled to someone, we risk never getting around to doing it. We must redeem the time by "making the most of every opportunity, because the days are evil" (Ephesians 5:15).

Inside The Wall
Reconciling strained relationships should not stop once you have made things right with those you have wronged in society prior to your incarceration. It should include being reconciled to those you have wronged, or have been wronged by, that are also 'incarcerated' (Inside The Wall) be it a friend, an enemy, or anyone else you may have fallen out with at the facility you are housed at or at any other facility you were previously housed at.

Many of us have been wronged in some way by someone close to us, someone we trusted. It is an unfortunate fact of life that no one is exempt from. What matters, however, is how we choose to deal with a situation like that. If we choose to exact revenge, we choose the way that will cause a wider chasm than the one that already exists between us and that person. But if we choose to forgive and forget, we choose the way that honors God and opens the door for a blessing.

"Even my close friend whom I trusted, he who shared my bread, has lifted up his heel against me" (Psalm 41:9). This verse from the Old Testament of the Bible is a prophecy of Jesus' betrayal by Judas, and it was fulfilled in the New Testament (John 13:8, 26). As one of Jesus' twelve disciples, Judas spent three-years with the Master being taught by Him, traveling and eating with Him (Mark 3:14-19), and having charge of the group's treasury. Then he betrayed Jesus for thirty pieces of silver (Matthew 26:14-16).

"If you have ever been betrayed by someone close, then you know how Jesus must have felt when Judas betrayed Him. It was the mother of all betrayals!"

If you have ever been betrayed by someone close, then you know how Jesus must have felt when Judas betrayed Him. It was the mother of all betrayals! I too know how it feels to be betrayed by someone close. I had it done to me several times by people I was close to. In fact, two guys I was close to, guys I called "close friends", played a direct role in my having to spend a quarter of a century incarcerated. It took several years for me to forgive and forget their betrayal, and it was only because of God's love, mercy and grace that I was able to do so. Otherwise, I would still be carrying that baggage around with me to this day.

But today, because I have a relationship with my Creator and Savior, the Lord Jesus Christ, I can see these two guys, and others who have betrayed me, walking down the street and the thought of what they did to me will not even cross my mind. Because God forgave all my sins, I too must forgive others when they sin against me. It is a two-way street. *"For if you forgive men when they sin against you, your* heavenly Father will also forgive you. But if you do not forgive men their sins, your Father will not forgive your sins" (Matthew 6:14-15). "Forgive, and you will be forgiven" (Luke 6:37).

If there is anyone at your facility or at another facility (state or federal), or at a county jail whom you are at odds with, you should invest time making the effort to be reconciled to that person. "But I tell you that anyone who is angry at his brother will be subject to judgment" (Matthew 5:22). In His Divine wisdom that is the Lord Jesus Christ admonishing us about anger. We would be wise to take His heed!

Strained relationships hinder our relationship with God. Anger keeps us from developing a spirit pleasing to Him, because "...anger does not bring about the righteous life that God desires" (James 1:20). Whatever caused you to be at odds with whomever you have fallen out with, you should make the effort to quash it, as soon as time permits. It does not matter how deep the divide between you and the individual might be. The only thing that should matter is that you take the time and the initiative to right the wrong. If the other person will not make the first move, then you should take it upon yourself to be the bigger person and make that move.

"If anyone says, 'I love God,' yet hates his brother, he is a liar. For anyone who does not love his brother, whom he has seen, cannot love God, whom he has not seen. And he has given us this command: Whoever loves God must also love his brother" (1 John 4:20-21). Your relationship with God should be a reflection of your relationship with others. If it is not, then it is not genuine. God desires for us to love and be at peace with one another. "If it is possible, as far as it depends on you, live at peace with everyone. Do not take revenge, my friends, but leave room for God's wrath, for it is written: 'It is mine to avenge; I will repay,' says the Lord. On the contrary: 'If your enemy is hungry, feed him; if he is thirsty, give him something to drink. In doing this, you will heap burning coals on his head.' Do not be overcome by evil, but overcome evil with good" (Romans 12:18-21).

> *"Remember: forgiveness is a two-way street. It breaks the cycle of retaliation and bitterness and can lead to mutual reconciliation."*

I know this is possible because I did it. Not once or twice, but many times during my quarter of a century of incarceration. Turning the other cheek when someone wrongs you is not an easy thing to do; *it is the right thing to do!* Remember: forgiveness is a two-way street. It breaks the cycle of retaliation and bitterness and can lead to mutual reconciliation. Even if the person you fell out with never accepts your apology or apologizes for wronging you, by forgiving that person and forgetting whatever caused the falling out, you will be able to let go of that heavy burden you have been carrying and feel a sense of peace as a result.

Forgiving and forgetting is about attitudes and actions. If you want to get rid of your enemies, turn them into friends! The amount of time you invest during your incarceration reconciling strained relationships with those on the outside, as well as those on the inside, is an investment toward building new ones. It is also serving time productively.

BUILD NEW RELATIONSHIPS

Just as reconciling strained relationships is a productive way to serve time, so also is building new relationships. *"There is a time for everything, and a season for every activity under heaven: a time to tear down and a time to build"* (Ecclesiastes 3:1, 3). Establishing new relationships with inmates who are purpose driven and goal oriented can yield huge dividends in the near-term and long-term. In the near-term (during your incarceration) these relationships can help *you* stay focused on the positive and steer clear of the negative; in the long-term (when you are released), you will benefit from these relationships by having been able to sharpen your social skills. These skills will be useful to you when you are with your family, around co-workers or business associates, and meeting new people. You will need these skills to make a successful transition in society.

When I began serving time productively, I established genuine friendships with other inmates by seeking out those who were purpose-driven and goal-oriented and by avoiding those who were not. I would advise you to do the same with anyone who does not have your best interest at heart, unless of course you believe you can help them get on the right track so they too can serve their time in a productive manner. *"Don't be misled: Bad company corrupts good character"* (1 Corinthians 15:33). In order for me to stay purpose-driven and goal-oriented, I had to shed former partners-in-crime and make new partners-in-Christ. *"Do not set foot on the path of the wicked or walk in the way of evil men. Avoid it, do not travel on it; turn from it and go on your way. For they cannot sleep till they do evil; they are robbed of slumber till they make someone fall"* (Proverbs 4:14-16).

If you are serious about serving time productively and are determined never to return to a life of crime upon your release, you may have to do as I did by shedding old acquaintances and making new ones. *"He who walks with the wise grows wise, but a companion of fools suffers harm"* (Proverbs 13:20). *"Above all else, guard your heart, for it is the wellspring of life"* (Proverbs 4:23). *"Let your eyes look straight ahead, fix your gaze directly before you. Make level paths for your feet and take only ways that are firm. Do not swerve to the right or to the left; keep your foot from evil"* (Proverbs 4:25-27).

When building a new friendship or making a new acquaintance you have to know what kind of relationship you intend to establish with the other person, be it a friendship or acquaintance. A friend is someone you trust; an acquaintance is someone you associate with at a distance. One thing I learned when I began making new friends in prison was that I first had to be certain of the kind of friend I intended to be. *"A friend loves at all times, and a brother is born for adversity"* (Proverbs 17:17).

In the oftentimes unpredictable, hostile and backstabbing environment of a correctional facility, there is a sharp contrast between being a genuine friend and simply knowing a person. Again, you have to know what kind of relationship you intend to establish with that person. I believe the answer is quite simple: You should try to seek out positive friendships and acquaintances with people who will treat you as they would like to be treated. Mutual trust and respect are imperative in this equation. Most friendships end because of a lack of these essential relationship-building requirements.

The UNIVERSAL RULE formulated by Jesus Christ, the Master Builder of relationships says *"So in everything, do to others what you would have them do to you, for this sums up the Law and the Prophets"* (Matthew 7:12). In order to do this effectively, you must be willing to be there for a friend in times of distress or personal struggles just as you would expect for that friend to be there for you. A genuine friend who "loves at all times" is one who does as Jesus said *"Greater love has no one than this, that he lay down his life for his friends"* (John 15:13). Jesus laid down His life for us. That is how much He loved (and loves) us. His can be a difficult example to follow at times, but a good one.

You may not have to die for a friend, but you can show genuine friendship to him in other ways, i.e., lending him a helping hand however needed, taking time to listen, encouraging and advising; or giving something to your friend that they need. Those are but a few examples of how you can demonstrate true friendship. There are many more that I am certain you can think of on your own. Be creative and you will be amazed at the things you will come up with.

> *When you invest time being a genuine friend to a fellow inmate, you show that person the very heart of God.*

When you invest time being a genuine friend to a fellow inmate, you show that person the very heart of God. In Matthew 25:35-40, Jesus said *"For I was hungry and you gave me something to eat,*

I was thirsty and you gave me something to drink, I was a stranger and you invited me in. I needed clothes and you clothed me, I was sick and you looked after me, I was in prison and you came to visit me. Then the righteous will answer him, "Lord, when did we see you hungry and feed you, or thirsty and give you something to drink, or needing clothes and clothe you? When did we see you sick or in prison and go visit you?" The King will reply, 'I tell you the truth, whatever you did for one of the least of these brothers and sisters of mine, you did for me."

Jesus' point in this parable focuses on the importance of helping others in their time of need from right where you are. Such love and genuine concern for the well-being of others glorifies God by reflecting our love for Him. When you treat a fellow inmate as if he were Jesus, it shows what you really think about the Master's words. Your actions determine whether your friendship with those whom you befriend is genuine or fair-weather.

In a correctional setting, as in any setting, you will encounter many fair-weather people who will claim to be your friend. They will hang out with you as long as it benefits them, but will kick you to the curb as soon as it doesn't. That is why it is important to choose wisely whom you establish relationships with and to proceed with caution before you call a fellow inmate your friend. Take time to assess their true motives. It is better to be safe beforehand than to be sorry afterward. *"A simple man believes anything, but a prudent man gives thought to his steps"* (Proverbs 14:15).

During my incarceration, I was surrounded by guys who would not think twice about befriending a fellow inmate if they thought he was gullible and could use him for their own selfish purposes, whatever they might be. I am certain there are inmates serving time at your facility who are of that same mindset. Everyone who has a kind heart has had their kindness taken for granted at one time or another. It happened to me on several occasions, and it can happen to you. Play it safe: steer clear of inmates who come across as genuine, but are nothing more than wolves in sheep's clothing. *"By their fruit (actions) you will recognize them"* (Matthew 7:15-16, emphasis mine).

Serve your time productively by establishing friendships with inmates who are not fair-weather. Just as there are wolves in sheep's clothing looking for an unsuspecting inmate to befriend, so too there are inmates who will, by their "fruit", prove they are genuine. If you can read people fairly well, you will be able to detect a person's true character on the spot. When you meet a fellow inmate who is genuine, be as genuine to him as he is with you. *"Do to others as you would have them do to you"* (Matthew 7:12). A friendship that begins that way has the best chance of staying that way. This is the type of friendship that is worth investing time to establish.

Prison, as you already know, can be a lonely place. Just as there are inmates who feel lonely by being cut off from family and friends, there are inmates who do not have anyone on the outside and experience loneliness in ways that no one should ever have to. Being incarcerated adds to their loneliness. We all need friends who "will love at all times" and will lend an ear or a helping hand when we need it. These are friends who genuinely feel our pain and show their concern. They are there for us when things are going smoothly and especially when they are not.

I say "we" because people on the outside of those prison walls (or fences) need genuine friends as much as you who are incarcerated do. I needed genuine friends when I was incarcerated and that has not changed out here. I am still selective about the people I surround myself with. You have to be that way to avoid the wolves of the world, both in there and out here. It is better to have one genuine friend than one-hundred fair-weather acquaintances.

Do not just invest time looking for genuine friends, invest time being one. That is what establishing positive relationships is all about. If you are looking to build new friendships all you have to do is look around you. There are inmates who need a genuine friend. Ask God to reveal them to you, and when He does do your part by establishing a genuine friendship with them. *"A man of many companions may come to ruin, but there is a friend who sticks closer than a brother"* (Proverbs 18:29).

> *"Keep in mind that inmates who are not serving their time productively will steal your time if you allow them to. I dub them "time thieves".*

Keep in mind that inmates who are not serving their time productively will steal your time if you allow them to. I dub them "time thieves." Do your best to avoid them. I had to do that many times during the years I spent in prison serving time productively. There was always someone, whether it was an inmate or a staff member or both, who would start up a conversation about things that were neither productive nor beneficial to them or me and it always happened while I was working on something productive, or while I was in the gym or on the yard exercising. I was never short with anyone, but I had no problem letting these "time thieves" know I was busy and had to get back to whatever I was working on.

If you are serving time productively, you have probably had to thwart a few time thieves yourself and can relate to what I am saying. If you are not serving time productively but decide you want to after reading this book, be prepared to encounter time thieves of your own. Most of the time they do not even realize that they are infringing on your time, so you have two choices in a situation like that: allow them to steal your time or respectfully inform them you have business to tend to.

To be a successful time manager, you must develop the latter attitude, not only toward people who infringe on your time, but also toward places and things that can keep you stuck in a time freeze. That is exactly what I had to do. I acquired some haters because of it, but at the end of the day, I could say that I served my time productively. That is all that really mattered. Be wise and serve time productively by establishing productive friendships, and by being a genuine friend to those you befriend.

> *"One of the most important investments you can make in the area of time management during your incarceration has to do with making amends to the victim of your offense...or the victim's family."*

MAKE AMENDS TO THE VICTIM

One of the most important investments you can make in the area of time management during your incarceration has to do with making amends to the victim of your offense or, if you can't, to the victim's family. Although you may not be able to contact the victim of your offense directly to express how sorry you are for the hurt you caused them and their family, you might be able to do so through an attorney, if you have one, or, if you pleaded guilty, through the prosecutor.

If you are genuinely remorseful about the hurt you have caused, then express it in a letter. You may be surprised at how far a letter can go in getting the people you have hurt to forgive you. Victims of crime and sometimes their families have gone as far as to befriend the offender, visit him/her, and even stay in contact with him/her during their incarceration. However crazy that might sound, it does happen. That is the love, mercy, grace and forgiveness of God being displayed at its best.

I had a chance encounter with the brother of the victim in one of my cases while I was incarcerated. He was a few years younger than me. We met one day while I was delivering movement passes to inmates at the maximum security prison where I was housed at the time. As I passed a group of inmates in one of the prison corridors, one of them called out my name. I turned to ask if he knew me. He replied *"Hell yeah I know you. You killed my brother! You caught 'em snoozin' and he paid for it. The game is raw, but it's fair. I just wanted you to know I'm not trippin'"* To that I replied *"I appreciate that, lil' brother. We gotta live under the same roof for now, so we might as well be civil about it."* He agreed, we shook hands, and then we went our separate ways.

That was by far the craziest encounter I ever had in prison. But it was also one of the most civil I ever had with a member of an enemy gang. The encounter could have easily turned violent had he and his guys had violence on their minds that day. But by the grace of God, they did not. We crossed each other's paths again a few days later while on the main yard. I told him I was sorry for killing his brother. He reassured me there were no hard feelings on his part and hoped there were not any on mine, as his gang had killed members of my gang and he was himself serving a lengthy sentence for killing a member of my gang. I assured him in no uncertain terms that there were no hard feelings on my part either. The game was indeed raw, but it was also fair in it's own convoluted way.

The guy actually forgave me for killing his brother, which I am certain, took a lot on his part. We ended up becoming friends, even though it was at a distance because of our rival gang affiliation. It is a shame it had to be that way, but that was, and is, the "nature of the beast" (gang life). I did, however, befriend many other rival gang members during the latter years of my incarceration. All of us have long since retired from gang life. These are friends I consider "my brothers" by virtue of the fact that we are members of the same family, God's family! Our brotherhood-in-Christ was sealed by the blood of Christ when we accepted Him as our Savior and Lord. There is no greater brotherhood on earth than that; no brotherly-love more powerful.

> ### *"Remember those in prison as if you were their fellow prisoners" (Hebrews 13:3).*

Some of my brothers-in-Christ are still incarcerated and it hurts my heart because I know exactly what they are going through. I went through it for a quarter of a century. That is why I keep in touch with them and do whatever I can for them. *"Remember those in prison as if you were their fellow prisoners"* (Hebrews 13:3). That Scripture is the "motto" for my church's prison ministry, which I am proud to be a part of. I used to invest time keeping in touch with family, friends, and associates when I was incarcerated via correspondence, and now I invest time keeping in touch with people who are incarcerated, via correspondence, as part of my prison ministry duties. How awesome is that!

If you invest time during your incarceration to make amends to the victim of your offense, you will be doing a noble, moral and worthwhile deed. Not only will it prove that you are genuinely remorseful for the crime you committed and for the hurt you caused the victim and his or her family, but it will also prove that you have changed and are striving to be a better person. God can, and will, cause good to shine on an otherwise bad situation. *"And we know that in all things God works for the good of those who love him, who have been called according to his purpose."* (Romans 8:28) All you have to do is trust Him.

INVEST TIME IN YOUR CHILDREN

Another important investment of time you can make during your incarceration has to do with your children, if you have any. To those who do, God says *"Train a child in the way he should go, and when he is older he will not turn from it"* (Proverbs 22:6). You should not allow your circumstances or distance keep you from being involved in your children's lives, if you are able to. This is important, especially if they are young. You should do what you can to give them parental advice about staying on the right side of the law so they do not end up on the wrong side of it. You should do everything in your power to keep your children from ending up in the penal system.

You can serve time productively by investing quality time in your children's lives, and you can do it right where you are. If you have a good understanding with your children's other parent, particularly if you are still involved with her/him, you can stay involved in *their* lives as well by staying in contact with them via correspondence, email, phone calls, or visits, whichever of these you are fortunate enough to be blessed with, if not all of them. But even if you are not involved with your children's other parent anymore, you should still make the effort to stay involved in their lives. This is your God-given duty as a parent. Being incarcerated does not negate this in any way.

Leaving a child behind, particularly a young child, while you go off to serve prison time is a hard thing to do. I know what it is like not to be able to watch your children grow up, or to be there for them as a parent is supposed to be during those critical years while they are learning and their minds are developing, those all-important years when they need their parents the most. It is one of the hardest and most stressful things to endure when you are incarcerated. It is a helpless feeling. I experienced it firsthand, so I know.

I did not get the chance to raise my only son, to watch him grow from a toddler to a teenager and eventually to an adult. He was only two-years of age when I forfeited my freedom. I missed out on all the things a father and son are supposed to do together. Every time his mother or my parents sent me pictures of him, it would hit me hard and I would realize how much of his life I was missing out on, and just how much I had forfeited. It hurt a lot!

By the love, mercy and grace of God, I was fortunate enough to have a consistent relationship with my son throughout my incarceration. I give thanks to God for allowing my parents to be directly involved in my son's life. They practically raised him and made it possible for me to see him as often as possible. As a result, I was able to invest quality time with him via correspondence, phone calls and visits. The visits were the best but they also hurt the most, particularly when it was time for him to leave. It always felt like a part of me was leaving with him.

> *"Despite having to watch my son grow up in prison visiting rooms, I cherished those visits and give thanks to God for each one."*

I watched my son grow up in prison visiting rooms, not exactly the best environment to "teach a child in the way he should go", but a necessary one nonetheless for those who are incarcerated and have children and are able to visit with them. Despite having to watch my son grow up in prison visiting rooms, I cherished those visits and give thanks to God for each one. You should too, if you are fortunate enough to get visits from your children. You will be surprised at how much you can teach them and learn about them during those precious moments together. Even if your children are grown, still make the effort to invest time in their lives. Remember, it is your God-given duty.

Another important thing to be mindful of during your incarceration is the fact that you are confined to an environment where you have little, if any, control over your children's lives. If they are young and you are serving a sentence that may keep you incarcerated well into their teens or older, or if you are a lifer, then how your children turn out may not be something you can control, frustrating as that may be. I will use my son as a perfect example.

As with me when I was young, my son had no reason to embark on the destructive path he chose. He was only fourteen years old when he embarked on that path, the same age I was when I began to have run-ins with the law. I called home one day not long after my son began his freshman year in high school and was surprised when my parents informed me that he had been caught with some friends smoking marijuana at the school.

Up to that point, I had no idea whatsoever that my son had been involved in anything of that sort; neither did his mother or my parents. My son had been an "A" student all through his grade school years. How he went from being an "A" student to getting caught smoking marijuana at school was beyond me at the time. The fact that it happened made me realize just how little control his mom, and my parents and I, had in his young life.

I knew then that I had to invest more time trying to stay as involved in his life as possible, despite having twelve-years left to serve on my sentence. I did not, however, lose sight of the fact that there was only so much I could do to try to keep him on the straight and narrow from where I was. Yet, even my best efforts seemed to be in vain. His mother, and my parents and I, were losing control of his life. It was frustrating.

> *"Parenting is serious business and I had to be serious about the time I invested in my son's life regardless of my circumstances."*

When I say "control" I do not mean a demanding, domineering kind of control, but rather a loving, responsible, parental control that every parent should have over their children. I had to heed the Apostle Paul's instruction when he says, *"Fathers, do not exasperate your children; instead, bring them up in the training and instruction of the Lord"* (Ephesians 6:4). If I was not going to at least try to be a responsible parent, then I was not ready to be a parent and, therefore, had no right to get involved. Being incarcerated did not excuse me from this responsibility, nor did it negate my role as a parent. Parenting is serious business and I had to be serious about the time I invested in my son's life regardless of my circumstances.

I tried to do exactly that after the marijuana incident at school. But just when I thought my son had taken a turn for the better he threw me a curve ball, the kind that you cannot hit no matter how good your batting is. My father learned that he was in a gang, and not just any gang, but one of the biggest and most violent Latino gangs in Chicago. It gets worse. This gang just happened to be the main enemy of the gang I was once a member of. Imagine that!

Once I learned of this, I did everything I could to extricate my son from that lifestyle, because I knew how destructive it could be and I did not want him to end up in prison or worse, in an early grave, like I almost did. It is only by the love, mercy and grace of God that I lived through that violent and destructive period in my life. As much as it hurts to say it, prison actually saved my life. God allowed me to go through that twenty-four year hiatus so that I would not crash and burn. He had different plans for me and they did not include an early grave or a life sentence in prison. He also had different plans for my son and those plans did not include prison or an early grave. I just didn't know it at the time.

With all the negativity my son got himself involved in during his high school years, it is nothing short of a miracle that he managed to graduate when he was supposed to. For me it was like déjà vu. I barely managed to graduate from high school for the same reasons. Not only was my son smoking marijuana, he was drinking liquor and gang banging heavily as well. My main concern, prior to God delivering him from all that, was that he might end up in prison or worse, that he might not even live to see his eighteenth birthday.

In October of 2000, my son was arrested by Chicago Police Gang Intelligence Unit officers for possession of a loaded firearm and possession of narcotics with intent to deliver. In Illinois that is a Super-X felony that carries a sentence of 9-45 years if convicted, no probation. I immediately began making preparations for him to be transferred to the prison I was being housed at in the event that he was convicted. Yes, I was concerned that he would be convicted, given the fact that he was caught with the gun and drugs in his possession, and because his attorney advised him that if the judge denied their pretrial Motion to Suppress the Evidence, he would be going to prison.

Of course, God had different plans for him. Eight months later the case against him was dismissed. The judge granted his attorney's Motion to Suppress the Evidence on grounds that the officers did not have a valid reason to stop, detain, search, and arrest him. That is the mercy of God! In my spiritual opinion, the case was not dismissed because of *anything* my son or his lawyer did. It was dismissed because of God's *divine intervention.*

Talk about a stressful period. The thought of losing my only son to gang life, a life that almost destroyed me, weighed heavily on my spirit. Fortunately, I serve an awesome God! As with me it is only by the love, mercy and grace of God that my son did not end up in prison and is alive and well today. The streets could have easily swallowed him up as they almost did me.

You see, the time I invested in my son's life during my incarceration, particularly during the years he spent on the wrong side of the law, not only involved correspondence, phone calls, and visits; but also a lot of intercessory prayer being made on his behalf as well. God heard and answered every one of those prayers according His perfect will. *"The prayer(s) of a righteous man are powerful and effective"* (James 5:16).

My son decided it was time to get his act together soon after that. In 2002, after discussing the matter with me and his mother, he decided to enlist in the military, an experience he feels helped turn his life around for the better despite America being at war in Iraq and Afghanistan, and military life being what it is. He has served his country honorably and bravely and has no regrets whatsoever. He honorably discharged from the military the same year I discharged from parole.

I believe everything happens at the appointed time, according to God's purpose and plan. The fact that my son was discharged from the military the same year I completed parole is evidence of that. God's timing is always perfect! The blessing is that I am out of prison and back in his life the way a father is supposed to be for his children, regardless of their age. I am here to love, encourage, and support him in every way that a parent should. We have plans to do big things together with God in the driver's seat.

I will never forget the day I was released from prison. My son was waiting for me on the steps of my mother's house. He hugged me and didn't want to let me go. I get teary-eyed just thinking of that moment; it was priceless! He keeps a picture of that moment as the wallpaper on his laptop. I love it! My wife has three children as well, all of whom are grown and have known my son since they were kids. We also have seven grandkids.

"Children's children are a crown to the aged, and parents are the pride of their children" (Proverbs 17:6). My wife and I are blessed to be parents and grandparents.

To those who have children, I encourage you to take advantage of every opportunity you have to invest quality time in their lives during and after your incarceration. It is truly one of the best investments of time you can make for *"Sons are a heritage from the LORD; children are a reward from him. Like arrows in the hands of a warrior are sons born in one's youth. Blessed is the man whose quiver is full of them... "* (Psalm 127:3-5)

Do you want to serve time productively? Then invest quality time in your children's lives. Not only is it your God-given duty, it is an investment that you will receive a priceless return on both during and after your incarceration. It's also a good way to improve your social skills.

TRAIN YOURSELF TO BECOME AN EFFECTIVE COMMUNICATOR AND LISTENER

One of the most effective ways to serve time productively is to improve your social skills. The best way to do this is to sharpen your communication skills, i.e., reading, writing, comprehension, speech, and listening. Effective communication, however, particularly in a correctional setting, can be somewhat difficult and, at times, dangerous. Oftentimes, the message being conveyed is not always the message being received. A number of factors can play into that, among them, body language.

Even when clearly stated, words can be misinterpreted or misunderstood. This is especially true when words are filtered through the sieve of prejudices or misconceptions. The Bible gives us many examples of wise and foolish communication. Consider the following verses in the book of Proverbs:

> *"A man finds joy in giving an apt reply—and how good is a timely word."* - Proverbs 15:23

> *"A man's heart guides his mouth, and his lips promote instruction"* - Proverbs 16:23

> *"A man of knowledge uses words with restraint, and a man of understanding is even-tempered. Even a fool is thought wise if he keeps silent, and discerning if he holds his tongue."* - Proverbs 17:27-28

> *"A fool's mouth is his undoing, and his lips are a snare to his soul."* - Proverbs 18:7

> *"From the fruit of his mouth a man's stomach is filled; with the harvest of his lips he is satisfied."* - Proverbs 18:20

> *"While it is important to have something positive to say, it is equally important to know what to say, when to say it, and how to say it."*

Wise people weigh carefully what they say, when they say it, and how they say it; foolish people don't because they could care less about the effects their words might have. While it is important to have something positive to say, it is equally important to know what to say, when to say it, and how to say it. This calls for wisdom (James 1:5).

In an environment as unpredictable as prison, it is important to pause to think before you speak. I had to heed that advice many times during my incarceration. If I had not during those times when I was confronted with situations that could have easily turned violent, I probably would not have made it out of prison when I was supposed to. My mouth would have been my undoing and I would have myself to blame for not choosing my words more carefully.

"He who guards his mouth and his tongue keeps himself from calamity" (Proverbs 21:23). That is exactly what I had to train myself to do, but once I did, it humbled me to the point where it was hard for anyone to verbally pull me off my square. Did that come easily for me? Absolutely not! I first had to let go of the gang member bravado mentality I had allowed myself to be indoctrinated with for fifteen years. With the help of the Holy Spirit, I was able to delete that negative character flaw once and for all.

In Matthew 21:33, the Lord Jesus Christ warns us of the danger of misusing words: "But I tell you that men will have to give an account on the day of judgment for every careless word they have spoken. For by your words you will be acquitted, and by your words you will be condemned."

Consider the following verses in the Book of James:

"If anyone considers himself religious and yet does not keep a tight rein on his tongue, he deceives himself and his religion is worthless" - James 1:26

"The tongue also is a fire, a world of evil among the parts of the body. It corrupts the whole person, sets the whole course of his life on fire, and is itself set on fire by hell. All kinds of animals, birds, reptiles, and creatures of the sea are being tamed by man, but no man can tame the tongue. It is a restless evil, full of deadly poison. With the tongue we praise our Lord and Father, and with it we curse men, who have been made in God's likeness. Out of the same mouth come praise and cursing. My brothers, this should not be" - James 3:6-10)

"Everyone should be quick to listen, slow to speak and slow to become angry, for man's anger does not bring about the righteous life that God desires" - James 1:19-20

So, if your social skills are lacking because your communication skills aren't up to par, then it's time to invest time improving this important area of your life.

In early 1992, after spending the previous eight-years of my incarceration with my head dug in the sand, I decided it was time to get back in school and educate myself as much as I possibly could. I knew it was not going to be easy given the fact that I had all but lost interest in academics. I had allowed my mind to become indoctrinated with the negativity of gang life, which led me to adopt an attitude of "I'm not interested in anything in here except getting out!" That is something you do NOT want to do during your incarceration.

This type of attitude will eventually lead you to engage in destructive behavior that will eventually get you caught up and may even prolong your stay in prison, if not indefinitely! All you have to do is look around you to see how many inmates have needlessly fallen into that dead-end trap. You are currently reading the words of an ex-inmate that it almost happened to.

> *"Being incarcerated around other inmates who lived and breathed gang life 24-7 did nothing for me during the eight-years I mismanaged except make me more of a hardened criminal."*

Being incarcerated around other inmates who lived and breathed gang life 24-7 did nothing for me during the eight-years I mismanaged except make me more of a hardened criminal. My entire mindset during that time centered on a foolish plan to circumvent the rules and regulations of the Illinois prison system for the duration of my forty-eight-year sentence, not allow anyone or anything to stop me from being released on my release date, and then return to Chicago with a renewed focus and determination to transform the gang I was a member of into the most sophisticated, most powerful, and most ruthless criminal organization in America. I wasn't just going to reenter society, I was going to bum rush it!

That foolish plan, however realistic it might have seemed to me at the time, never materialized. I give thanks to God that it didn't or I might have ended up back in prison, quite possibly serving a life sentence at the federal Super-Max in Florence, Colorado, or be dead by now. It is also certain that you would not be benefitting from the Godly wisdom you are receiving in the area of managing time in a correctional setting by reading this book.

So what helped me flip from being a gang banging, drug dealing, streetwise thug who thought he was "all that" - but in actuality was lost and wandering aimlessly - to being a God-fearing man who now lives his life according to God's purpose and plan? More than anything, it was and is my relationship with the Lord Jesus Christ.

Once I rededicated my life to the Lord, I took a 180-degree turn and everything began to work out for the good. *"And we know that in all things God works for the good of those who love him, who have been called according to his purpose"* (Romans 8:28). I stopped conforming myself to the pattern of this world and was transformed by the renewing of my mind (Romans 12:1-2).

This, however, did not happen overnight. This was, and still is, a spiritual process that takes place one day at a time. For *"he who began a good work in you will carry it on to completion until the day of Christ Jesus"* (Philippians 1:6). I am a spiritual work in progress. Everyone who accepts Jesus Christ as their Lord and Savior is, too.

I began to take college classes again after that eight-year period of mismanaged incarceration. A period where time that did me, instead of me doing it. I set goals for myself, one of which centered on getting a college degree. Reading became my out. It was the catalyst that motivated me to study hard, learn everything I could about the subject matter of each course I took, and to get the best grades possible. I managed to maintain a very respectable 3.4 G.P.A. (grade point average).

I invested as much time as I could reading everything I could get my hands on. My goal with reading was to be well-versed in as many life-relevant subjects as possible (i.e., theology, politics, health, philosophy, psychology, sociology, business, finance, commerce, real estate, sports, law, science, to name a few) so that I would be able to hold a conversation with anyone, anywhere, at any time, in any or all of those subjects. I wanted to be able to do this not just while I was incarcerated, but more so after my release.

Having learned as much as I could about each of these subjects armed me with knowledge. Not only so that I would know what I was talking about when holding a conversation with someone, but so that I would be able to comprehend others when they spoke on any of these subjects. The time I invested reading during my incarceration was time served productively because the dividends paid off profitably in the near-term (during my incarceration) and in the long-term (after my incarceration).

One of the dividends I received during my incarceration was the enhancement of my vocabulary. While studying for my Associates degree, I noticed after asking God to help me delete profanity and slang from my vocabulary, that I began to decrease my use of street slang (or "slangish," as I like to call it...I have a copyright on that word, so don't even think about it! lol) that I had been accustomed to speaking.

I began to speak English for the first time without the use of slang. In fact, my ability to speak English properly improved so much that I was able to turn my use of slang on and off at will. I was committed to changing that part of my life and I did. I still speak "slangish" at times, but only when I am speaking to someone whose vocabulary is laden with it, as mine once was, and only so that I do not lose that person by speaking words that he or she might not otherwise understand.

> **"We can bless or curse others with our words...I wanted to bless, not curse others. So that's what I began doing...I still do to this day"**

I also stopped using profanity. This was a *must* if I was going to *"Let no unwholesome talk come out of my mouth, but only what is helpful for building others up according to their needs, that it may benefit those who listen"* (Ephesians 4:29). We can bless or curse others with our words. I wanted to bless, not curse, others. So that's what I began doing with my newfound vocabulary. I still do to this today.

One of the tools that helped me enhance my vocabulary was an English dictionary and thesaurus. Every time I came across a word in one of my college textbooks or some other book that I could not pronounce, or did not know the definition of, I would look it up in my dictionary/thesaurus. I kept a Webster's dictionary/thesaurus with me whenever I was doing homework or working on an essay or some other writing project.

I learned how to pronounce and use words I had never spoken before, words I never imagined I would use in a conversation with anyone or in any of my writings. As a result of the time I invested during my incarceration reading and training myself to speak more proficiently, I went from being an under educated person who only knew how to speak "slangish" and cursed like a drunken sailor, to one who is educated, listens intently, speaks proficiently, and can't even stand to hear profanity. That is God's handiwork.

Give Him something to work with and He will come right alongside you to help you bring that thing to fruition. He did it for me more times than I can count and in many different ways, and He continues to do it. If you want examples, I can assure you that you're getting some just by reading this book. If He did it for me, He will do it for you if you lack basic reading skills and are serious about investing time during your incarceration to improve your vocabulary. The amount of time you invest will determine the return on your investment.

Not only does reading improve your vocabulary, but the more time you invest doing it the more you feed the one thing that prison cannot imprison: YOUR MIND! Therefore, I encourage you to invest time reading as much as you can. You can never read too much. The more knowledge you acquire, the more you will be able to understand this complex world we live in. This will go a long way toward enabling you to become socially responsible both during and after your incarceration.

If you are going to be released sometime in the near future and desire to be socially responsible in the community you are being paroled to, it is imperative that you have at least a basic understanding of the way life actually works. Not life as you knew it prior to your incarceration (that way of life is what landed you in prison), but life as a God-fearing, law-abiding citizen, the kind of citizen your neighbors will not have a problem living next door to.

If after reading many books that can help you gain that kind of knowledge you still have questions regarding life-relevant issues, try reading the Bible. It is hands down the best book you will ever read. It is life's Instruction Manual (Basic Instructions Before Leaving Earth) and it is the only book that will answer any and every question you might have about life, its purpose and meaning, and your role in it during your pilgrimage on Earth.

It did that for me during my incarceration and continues to do that for me every day of my life. I have a close relationship with God, because I invest time in prayer and in His Word. I could not live life successfully without investing time in prayer and studying the Word of God, because I would not be living; I would just be existing. Who wants to live like that? I sure don't! If you do not know how to read, now is a good time to invest time to learn. The near-term and long-term benefit to you cannot even be measured in words.

> *"Writing is by far one of the most valuable skills an inmate can have during and after his/her incarceration."*

WRITING

This is by far one of the most valuable skills an inmate can have during and after his/her incarceration. If used wisely, writing can be one of the most productive ways to serve time while incarcerated. It allows you to express yourself in ways you might not feel comfortable doing verbally. Some inmates may never realize they have a gift, talent, or skill for writing. Others who know they have it have never taken the time to develop it, or simply do not care to utilize it for one reason or another.

I never knew I had this gift until 1992, when George W. Knox, Ph.D., a Professor of Sociology at Chicago State University, befriended me after I wrote him a letter expressing interest in a book he had written about gangs, visited me at the facility I was housed at. After sharing some of my former gang life experiences with him, he suggested I write a memoir. He then offered to plug the book, once the manuscript was completed, as a "forthcoming book" in the gang research publication he is the Editor-in-Chief of, a very nice gesture coming from someone who barely knew me. Not only is Dr. Knox one of the country's leading experts on gangs, he's also a genuinely nice person, one I have a great deal of respect and admiration for.

God blessed me by sending Dr. Knox to me when He did. I informed Dr. Knox that I had no experience writing a book and would not even know how or where to start. He advised me to go as far back as I could remember and start writing from there; not to concern myself with spelling or punctuation, and to just write my story as if I were telling it verbally, the way I shared it with him. So, that is exactly what I did.

The first draft of my manuscript was a handwritten, 100-page chronology of events in my life from the time I became a gang member at age twelve, until I hung up my colors and walked away from gang life some fifteen years later. The first draft read terribly! Not one to do anything half-heartedly, I decided to learn as much as I could about writing before writing the second draft of the manuscript. After investing quality time (about three-months) reading a variety of books on writing and becoming familiar with different writing formats and styles, I felt I was ready to rewrite the manuscript.

The only problem was by then I had lost my desire to rewrite the manuscript in handwritten form. I wanted to type the manuscript but did not know how to type, so I decided to put my book project on hold until I learned how to type. Fortunately, I was able to purchase an electric typewriter from the inmate commissary, a Canon TypeStar II with liquid crystal display and all kinds of other cool features, including a built-in practice typing program. Typewriters are pretty much obsolete now, but that typewriter was a gem to me back then. God is good!

It took all of two-weeks for me to learn how to type a minimum of 45 words-per-minute, not bad for someone who did not know how to type just two-weeks earlier. I immediately began rewriting the manuscript. I enjoyed the time I invested working on the manuscript so much that writing became my second out; reading was my first. Aside from the other activities that I made part of my daily routine, I invested a minimum of four hours a day (two in the afternoon and two in the evening) working on my manuscript. It was not until ten years and 1,393 pages later that I finally decided it was time to finish the story and write the epilogue.

If you are wondering why it took ten years to complete the manuscript, it is because my story did not end the year I walked away from gang life. I chose to incorporate other events that continued to transpire afterward, and still other events that were transpiring in the lives of some of the individuals directly related to the story. I even wrote the last chapter to coincide with events I envisioned playing out once I was released, which is something I gave serious thought to even though I still had six years left to serve.

As for the manuscript itself, well, that is another story. Although the manuscript attracted a lot of attention in New York, suffice it to say the editor who was assigned to review the sample chapters I submitted to his publisher, a top-tier publisher mind you, decided to pass on the manuscript for reasons that are not even worth stating. I will say, however, that at first I was upset with the whole process. As time went on I chose to leave it alone and move forward because it was water under the bridge. I had more productive things to do with my time than to dwell on "would've, could've, should've".

If you are ever confronted with a situation like that do not allow it to frustrate you. Accept the situation for what it is, or as the Bible says "...*consider it pure joy...*" (James 1:2). Then put it behind you and move forward. That is what I did. It is a prime example of having good social skills, which is what this chapter is all about.

The time I invested in the manuscript was not a waste; nothing is wasted with God. Not only did it keep me from getting myself caught up in all the drama that occurred during that ten-year period at the facility I was housed at, but I was able to sharpen my writing skills and become a professional writer, though I humbly admit I have yet to master this priceless talent. Even so, I had a lot of fun writing that manuscript. I had the chance to relive events in my mind and learn a valuable lesson from mistakes I had made in the past; mistakes I am determined never to make again.

> *"God...has always managed to bring something good out of bad situations I have encountered, for that is who He is and that is what He does..."*

Not once has God failed me. He has always managed to bring something good out of bad situations I have encountered, for that is who He is and that is what He does (Genesis 50:20). The good that came out of all the work I put into the manuscript over that ten-year period, even though it did not get published, unfolded in several ways as a result of the talent God blessed me with.

I submitted a short story, formerly a chapter from my manuscript that did not get published, to an author named Jeff Evans who was putting together an anthology of writings from prisoners across the United States. Out of 400-plus submissions, he selected mine along with thirty-six others to include in his book. The book is entitled

Undoing Time: American Prisoners in Their Own Words. It is a must-read. If you have not read it, I encourage you to get a copy. It's also available as an e-book for those of you who are not incarcerated and own a Kindle or a Nook.

In addition to my writing accomplishments (however small they might seem), a proposal was made to me by Jeff Evans, who befriended me as a result of our collaboration on *Undoing Time* and on my memoirs. He advised me to nix the memoir and use the hard-hitting material as fodder for a television series that he believed had the potential to become the next big thing on television, post-*Sopranos*.

Jeff pitched the idea to me by explaining that such a project could actually become a hit if packaged and marketed correctly. He did not have to make his pitch twice. I was sold. This became my next writing project. I invested time during the latter years of my incarceration drafting the outline and creating the characters. The rest of what is commonly called a "series bible" needs to be drafted before I can start shopping it around. I am excited about this project simply because I believe once it is produced it will change the face of television as we know it. I am calling things that be not as though they were (Romans 4:17). That is faith, plain and simple.

In August 2005, with a little under three-years left to serve on my forty-eight year sentence, I had all but run out of ideas for writing projects. Then, as I explained earlier, while walking the yard one day, the idea for the book you are holding in your hands came to me. I believe God directed me to write this book because He foreknew that inmates in jails and prisons across America and the rest of the world would benefit from it. I immediately put pen to paper.

After spending a few weeks jotting down a rough draft for the book, I began writing the manuscript. It took eight months to complete. I did not begin writing the second draft until after my release. It took thirteen months to complete the second draft because I had other responsibilities at the time aside from the manuscript. It then took several more years and lots of proof reading and editing to get this book published.

Both the television series project and the book you are holding were worthwhile investments of time for me during those latter years of my incarceration. I believe they will continue to be for many years to come. God gets all the credit for this.

When you invest time writing during your incarceration, you serve time productively. If you do not know how to write, I encourage you to invest time learning, developing, cultivating, and utilizing this valuable skill, if you have not already. Hook up with someone at your facility who will invest time of their own to teach you the basics. If you cannot find anyone, do not let that deter you. Spend time at the library reading books you can use to teach yourself. If I did it, so can you. So can anyone for that matter!

Whether or not you know how to write, the amount of time you invest learning this skill, and developing, cultivating, and utilizing it will be time served productively. At the end of the day, writing can be an effective way to improve your social skills.

> *"I learned early in life, when I was running the streets, that in order to have good communication skills, you must have good comprehension skills."*

COMPREHENSION

Not only are reading and writing essential to improving your social skills, but so is comprehension. I learned early in life, when I was running the streets, that in order to have good communication skills, you must have good comprehension skills. In order to have good comprehension skills, you have to be a good listener. *"Everyone should be quick to listen"* (James 1:19).

When you have good comprehension skills, you are able to understand everything you read or hear. You are able to comprehend what something means or what someone says. This is important because there are people who do not always follow logic when expressing their views, which can lead to confusion. It is easy to make statements or write essays that are based on information that does not always convey the truth or state the facts. This often happens when a person tries to influence or sway the opinions of his audience. This is why it is important to be able to comprehend everything you read or hear. No one likes to be misled. I certainly don't! This did not change after I was released from prison.

One indication of good comprehension is the ability to recognize when someone is trying to influence you in a way that is either good or bad. In society, it is important to know this, particularly if you are on parole. In a correctional setting, it is a matter of life and death! This is something I never lost sight of during my incarceration, and neither should you.

I served the first eight years of my sentence in the company of Illinois' most dangerous felons. I was one of them. The art and science of "reading" inmates well was not just an instinct, it was a necessity. I was able to distinguish within the first five minutes of meeting someone new if he was genuine or phony. If he was the former, I would embrace him; if he was the latter, I would avoid him unless he was willing to flip the script and be real.

Reading people well is not something I picked up in prison. It is a God-given gift called "discernment." I knew I had the ability to discern things long before I ever saw the inside of a prison. It is a gift that can be used for good or bad purposes. I used it many times during my fifteen years of gang life on the streets and in prison. I interacted with a lot of shady characters during that time and I'm thankful for the discernment I had.

I dubbed prison "the devil's real estate" because that is exactly how I viewed it at one time. Career felons, as I once was, created and fostered that type of environment in prison. God is no respecter of persons, and neither are most people. There are inmates today who fit that description, who have no love or respect for life. If that is you, then now is a good time to flip that script. Not only for your sake, but for the sake of those you have to serve time with.

In order for you to know whether someone is trying to influence you in a good way or bad way, your comprehension level has to be up to par. The amount of time you invest sharpening your comprehension skills will help you to increase your knowledge and understanding of the way the world really works. You will also be improving your social skills in the process.

> *"...invest as much time as possible during your incarceration improving your comprehension skills. You will benefit from this in your interaction with inmates and staff alike."*

For this reason I encourage you to invest as much time as possible during your incarceration improving your comprehension skills. You will benefit from this in your interaction with inmates and staff alike. They will respect you more if you come across as someone who cannot be taken advantage of because you can read people well. Moreover, if you are perceived this way by those you interact with during your incarceration, when you are released, the people you come in contact with in society (be it family, relatives, co-workers, business associates, etc.) will also perceive you this way.

Whether you are soon to be released or not, by investing time improving your comprehension skills via the written and spoken word, your social skills will greatly increase and you will be better prepared to understand everything you read or hear.

PEOPLE SKILLS

How well do you get along with others? How tolerant are you of others character flaws? How do you respond when others irk you in some way? Do you work well with others, or do you prefer to work alone? Are you an introvert or an extrovert? How you answer these simple, yet, important questions can have a profound impact on your life both during and after your incarceration.

In order to have good social skills, you must be a people person. You must be able to treat others as you would have them treat you (Luke 6:31). You must be able to get along with others regardless of their character flaws. You must be able to respond kindly when someone treats you badly. You must be able to work well with others.

"But I tell you who hear me: Love your enemies, do good to those who hate you, bless those who curse you, pray for those who mistreat you" (Luke 6:27-29). If you feel that your present environment is a difficult place to be social, you are not alone. I felt that way many times throughout my incarceration, yes, even after I accepted Christ! Walking in God's love, mercy, grace, compassion and forgiveness toward certain inmates and staff that used to rub me the wrong way was not an easy thing for me to do, but it was essential if I wanted God to show me love, mercy, grace, compassion, and forgiveness.

However, it was not until I discovered who I really was, the person God created me to be and began to develop social skills that I was able to treat the inmates and staff who rubbed me the wrong way in a Christ like manner. Doing this enabled me to view even those I once considered my enemies in a different light; one that did not include wanting to cause them bodily harm. Instead I viewed them through the eyes of Christ, the eyes of love, for God is love (1 John 4:8, 16).

Because of God's love, I was able to establish and maintain genuine friendships with guys who were once my most hated enemies. *"When a man's ways are pleasing to the LORD, he makes even his enemies to be at peace with him"* (Proverbs 16:9). In doing so, I had to acknowledge something that for years I had all but ignored: that more often than not, those who do not have your best interest at heart are not always your enemies, but those you call your friends. Forget about brotherhood being universal, it was not even local at any of the facilities I was housed at, including the Cook County Jail.

Being confined in an environment such as a correctional facility for a prolonged period of time can make you immune to the violence and negativity that goes on in prison daily *if* you allow yourself to become insensitive to it. God had to open my eyes to the reality that I was in an environment where certain men simply had no love for Him, and they certainly would not have any for me. When God did open my eyes to this reality, instead of letting it consume my thoughts, by faith I accepted it for what it was and moved on.

Instead of distancing myself from these inmates (which my human nature wanted me to do) I chose not to be critical of them and instead embraced them with love, mercy, grace, compassion, and forgiveness. God did that for me when I was lost and wandering aimlessly, so it was my duty as a Christian to treat these inmates the same way: in a Christ-like manner. That is exactly what I did, even though most of them never reciprocated. I was able to relate to these guys because I saw in them some of the same character flaws I had in me prior to walking away from gang life: distrust, malice, deceit, hate, anger, to name a few.

It would have been nothing short of hypocrisy to judge them for carrying themselves the way I once did. To avoid doing that, I chose to heed the words of the Lord Jesus when He said *"Why do you look at the speck of sawdust in your brother's eye and pay no attention to plank in your own eye? How can you say to your brother, 'Let me take the speck out of your eye,' when all the time there is a plank in your own eye? You hypocrite, first take the plank out of your own eye, and then you will see clearly to remove the speck from your brother's eye"* (Matthew 7:3-5).

Powerful words, aren't they? Had I ignored Christ's admonition, I would have done so at my own peril. I chose to take heed instead.

> *"Bear in mind that if you are judgmental of others, be it friend or foe, you will be opening the door for others to be judgmental of you."*

Bear in mind that if you are judgmental of others, be it friend or foe, you will be opening the door for others to be judgmental of you. If you show love, mercy, grace, compassion, and forgiveness, the same will come back to you in full measure. *"For with the measure you use, it will be measured to you"* (Luke 6:38).

When the Lord Jesus Christ, the Author of love, mercy, grace, compassion, and forgiveness, gave us the admonishment in Luke 6:27-28, and 31, He was giving us clear instructions on how we should treat others. In Matthew 7:3-5, He did not tell us to overlook wrongdoing. He admonished us about judging other people while overlooking our own faults. We think we are better than others when we judge them, when in fact no one on this planet is better than the next person. If anything, God expects us to *"…consider others better than ourselves"* (Philippians 2:3).

It does not matter what a person's status in life is, either. God is no respecter of persons. That is why He created us equal. *"You, therefore, have no excuse, you who pass judgment on someone else, for at whatever point you judge the other, you are condemning yourself, because you who pass judgment do the same things"* (Romans 2:1). Instead of criticizing or judging others over whatever might irk you about them, be mindful of your own character flaws.

Your current environment is not a difficult place to try to be social. In fact, a correctional setting can be one of the easiest places to be social. Here are two reasons why: (1) You are in a socially-rich environment surrounded by people, both inmates and staff; (2) You have time to be social, or at best, learn how to be social.

The more time you invest developing this skill during your incarceration, the better you will become at displaying it. This important character trait will benefit you during your incarceration by helping you gain the respect of those around you and minimize the chance of you getting caught up in prison drama. When you are released, it will carry over into your relationships with family, friends, colleagues, co-workers, and whoever else God chooses to place in your life. You will have foreknowledge of how to conduct yourself around others, and people will gravitate toward you because of it.

For those of you who are not being released any time soon, and especially those who are "lifers", you too can benefit from having good social skills, if you don't already, by applying them during your incarceration. In doing so, God can use you as an instrument of His will to promote peace and harmony wherever you might find yourself throughout the course of your incarceration. That is precisely what He did with me, even though from time to time I had to contend with inmates who had no love or respect for God or people.

You too will encounter inmates throughout the course of your incarceration who choose to carry themselves that way. You probably already have. It is a fact of prison life, unfortunate as it might be. Nevertheless, God loves them in spite of their hateful ways, and so should you because *"He causes his sun to rise on the evil and the good, and sends his rain on the righteous and the unrighteous"* (Matthew 5:45). That is how I chose to carry inmates whose minds were stuck on folly. I did not kill them with kindness; I just displayed it to them every chance I got.

At the end of the day, you alone must choose whether you want to serve your time being at peace or at odds with the inmates and staff at your facility. Why add to the difficulty of being incarcerated by being at odds with those you're incarcerated with? Why not instead *"Bless those who persecute you; bless and do not curse. Rejoice with those who rejoice; mourn with those who mourn. Live in harmony with one another. Do not be proud, but be willing to associate with people of low position. Do not be conceited. Do not repay anyone evil for evil. Be careful to do what is right in the eyes of everybody. If it is possible, as far as it depends on you, live at peace with everyone"* (Romans 12: 14-18). This is one of the most stress-free ways to serve time. It is how I chose to serve time once I learned how to manage it.

COMMUNITY-BASED ORGANIZATIONS (CBO'S)

Once you invest time learning and applying social etiquette in your relationships by improving your communication and people skills, the next logical step to take during your incarceration, so that you can continue serving time productively, should be to start making contact with community-based organizations (or CBO's as I call them) that are committed to helping inmates during and after their incarceration. That is, if you have not already taken that step.

> **"God did not put us on this earth to serve ourselves. He put us here to serve Him and others."**

"Two are better than one, because they have a good return for their work: If one falls down, his friend can help him up. But pity the man who falls and has no one to help him up" (Ecclesiastes 4:9-10).

God did not put us on this earth to serve ourselves. He put us here to serve Him and others. You serve God when you serve others.

As such, there can be many benefits to investing time during your incarceration by networking with a CBO. You will not only meet new people that can help you, and whom you can help in some way during your incarceration, but you can begin to lay a positive foundation for your eventual release, one that can help you make a successful transition in society and hopefully keep you from desiring a return to whatever landed you in prison; or anything criminal for that matter.

How do I know that networking with CBO's can be beneficial during and after your incarceration? I myself invested time during the latter years of my incarceration staying connected with a community-based Christian organization called Mission: USA. The benefit to me and them was mutual. They helped me during those latter years of my incarceration by ministering to my spiritual needs via correspondence, and I helped them upon my release by supporting their ministry as a volunteer and, when possible, financially. I made valuable contacts with people in the Chicagoland area through this ministry who are making a difference in the lives of many who have been released from prison. These people are committed to their ministry of helping ex-offenders and those caught up in the street life.

Although you are a convicted felon and will have to deal with that stigma when you are released, in God's eyes you are still unique and capable of fulfilling the purpose for which He created you. Being a convicted felon is merely a consequence of your past, one that cannot define or negate your future unless you allow it to. God loves you in spite of your past and wants to help you fulfill His preordained purpose for your life, but you have to be willing to allow Him, because he cannot and will not force you to do so. He already knows the plans that He has for you, plans to prosper you and not to harm you, plans to give you hope and a future (Jeremiah 29:11).

God alone knows every detail of our lives, including our beginning and our end. He reveals our purpose to us and sees to it that we are able to fulfill it. We can rest assured that we will not fail, because He will not fail us. God has not failed me even once; not while I was incarcerated or since my release from prison.

This does not mean we will not experience trials, hardships, pain, or suffering during the course of our lives, but that our all-knowing, all-powerful, and ever-present Creator will be with us every step of the way to *"Instruct us and teach us in the way we should go; to counsel us, and watch over us"* (Psalm 32:8). God Himself goes before us and will be with us; He will never leave us nor forsake us. So we do not have to be afraid or discouraged (Deuteronomy 31:8).

God does not expect us to fulfill our calling on our own. That is precisely why He already has people in place waiting to help you during and after your incarceration, people who are committed to their respective calling. God will do His part by providing you with resources, people, skills, finances, etc., but you must do your part by appropriating those resources and utilize them in ways that are conducive to fulfilling your God-given purpose. Working with those whom God places in your path to help you is an excellent way to ensure you are doing that. It is also a productive way to manage time during and after your incarceration.

> *"In order for a community to function at its best, it needs people who are committed to building, maintaining and protecting its interests."*

In order for a community to function at its best, it needs people who are committed to building, maintaining and protecting its interests. Whatever community you plan to reside in when you are released, that will be *your* community, and that community needs you. Do not allow anyone to tell you that you have nothing to contribute; every ex-offender has something to contribute.

It is imperative, therefore, that you invest time during your incarceration establishing contacts with CBO's in the community you plan to reside in. Ask God to lead you to the organization(s) He wants you to get involved with. The Holy Spirit will confirm to you which one(s). Establish a relationship built on trust with someone at the organization(s) you are lead to get involved with. Once you establish trust with someone in the organization, ask how you can contribute your time, gifts, skills, talents, and/or finances, (if you can contribute financially).

Even if you are not going to be released in the near future, do not let that deter you from pursuing this. You can still make a valuable contribution to a CBO from where you are. God is not limited by time or space. He can use you whether you have a release date or not; all you have to do is let Him. He promises to do His part, but you have to be willing to do your part.

There are inmates in correctional facilities across this country that can use all the help they can get, but most do not know who to seek help from. Even if they do, they hesitate to ask, because they do not know how to approach them, or are concerned about being denied.

If you are seeking help of some kind, do not let the fear of being denied keep you from contacting a CBO that is most able to help you. If you do not know who exactly to contact, ask your counselor if he or she can provide you with an updated list of CBO's located in your state, particularly in the community where you plan to reside upon your release. You can also try to obtain that information from the librarian or a law clerk at your facility's library. If nothing else, you can ask someone on the outside (family, relative, friend) to get this information for you on the Internet. Ask them to make sure that the contact information (name, address and phone number of each CBO) is up-to-date. Once you obtain the information, it is up to you to do the rest. The people who work for these organizations may be more approachable and interested in helping you than you think.

If you are serious about serving time productively so that you can make a successful transition in society when you are released, or if you are not being released anytime soon but desire to get involved with a CBO that can help you in some way during your incarceration, now is a good time to invest time establishing these contacts. For those being released soon, the benefit in establishing these contacts may be just what you need to help you stay focused on something positive for the duration of your incarceration and, more importantly, to keep you from reoffending once you are released.

If your release date is still years away, this can be a very productive way to serve your time. It was for me during the years I invested keeping in touch with that CBO. The return on that investment, however small it might seem, was huge, simply because I was able to serve God and others during some of my parole time as a volunteer.

Whether you are soon to be released or not, getting involved with a CBO that can help you in some way is a productive way to serve time and a beneficial resource to have. Everyone needs a little help, some more than others. The help you need is available, but it is up to you to seek it and use it wisely. Moreover, if you are serious about your relationship with God and intend to "walk that walk" when you are released, then I encourage you to contact faith-based CBO's that focus on the life skill needs of ex-offenders and provide essential support to empower successful re-entry in society.

"For those of you who are being released, there will be many opportunities to do volunteer work once you are out...invest time while incarcerated to "acquire the desire".

VOLUNTEER

For those of you who are being released, there will be many opportunities to do volunteer work once you are out. In order to be committed to such a noble endeavor in the free world, it is imperative that you invest time while incarcerated to "acquire the desire".

Let's keep it real, not everyone has the desire or the patience for volunteer work. In prison, it is almost unheard of because of the nature of the environment. Being incarcerated can sap most inmates of the desire to do anything good, meaningful, or worthwhile. Instead of being drawn toward that which is productive, there are inmates who, for any number of reasons, serve their time in an unproductive manner. If they are fortunate enough to be released, they will return to society unprepared for the challenges that await them.

The mindset of the inmate who has no desire to do anything good, meaningful, or worthwhile while incarcerated, though common among a certain segment of the inmate population in this country, does not reflect the whole. I know this because when I made the decision to flip the script and begin serving my time productively, I soon discovered that there were other inmates who desired to serve their time productively as well. I made it a point to surround myself with as many of them as possible.

While there are inmates who will laugh at you if you approach them about a volunteer opportunity at their facility, there are inmates (perhaps even you if you are reading this) that will jump at the opportunity to do volunteer work. Most will embrace the opportunity because they genuinely have a heart for it, while others will do it for whatever self-serving benefit they might receive. I do not advocate or encourage the latter. Whatever your motive may be for doing volunteer work, as long as it does not have anything to do with sabotaging the project at hand, then you should get involved. You will be doing something noble, and serving time productively as a result.

There are inmates who will shy away from volunteer work because in their minds there is no benefit, financial or otherwise, for them to get involved. That type of selfish attitude stems from *pride*, a destructive force that can keep inmates from doing anything good, meaningful or worthwhile, or from realizing their potential during and after their incarceration. In many instances, pride will drive an inmate to reoffend when he/she is released, and is one of the root causes of why the recidivism rate is so high (i.e., *"I'd rather go back to selling drugs than to work a nine-to-five job, or do volunteer work at a food pantry or homeless shelter"*).

If you are honest with yourself, you will admit that pride is the reason you are incarcerated. It was not until I was able to admit that to God, myself, and others that I was able to humble myself, flip the script, and begin to change for the better. If you desire to prosper and be successful in life, you first have to change your mindset from one of thinking negative and acting destructive, to one of thinking positive and acting constructive. You must be transformed by the renewing of your mind (Romans 12:1-2).

God cannot bless you and make you prosper you while you are serving the enemy of your soul. *"The thief (enemy, aka, Satan) comes only to steal and kill and destroy; I have come that they may have life, and have it to the full"* (John 10:10, emphasis mine). The "I" in this passage of Scripture is the Lord Jesus Christ; "they" refers to those who believe in Him.

As God in human form, Jesus was the most selfless volunteer ever to walk this earth. He helped those in need as an example to us who believe in Him, an example that is worth following. If you, during the time you have been incarcerated thus far, have not been able to admit to yourself and to God that pride was the cause of your downfall, then you are what I call "proud of heart" (*no disrespect intended; I too was proud of heart*). If this is you, then until you are able to admit that to yourself and to the Father, you will not be able to remove pride from your heart. If anything, you will continue to sink deeper into the abyss of negativity; quite possibly to the point of no return. If you think you are immune from that, think again (1 Corinthians 10:13).

I used to think that way too, but I found out the hard way that I was not. Such is the outcome of those who allow pride to control their mindset. I only wish I had taken heed to that sooner than later. I could have avoided a lot of unnecessary drama during those first eight years of my incarceration had I done so. Forget about being able to "acquire the desire" to involve yourself in anything good, meaningful or worthwhile, much less have a heart for noble causes such as volunteer work; it will not work as long as you are proud of heart. The Bible gives us repeated warnings about pride. Consider the following:

"The LORD detests all the proud of heart. Be sure of this:

they will not go unpunished." - Proverbs 16:5

"Pride goes before destruction, a haughty spirit before a fall." - Proverbs 16:18

"...God opposes the proud, but gives grace to the humble" - 1 Peter 5:5

Inmates who have a problem with pride refuse to admit they have this problem and tend to ignore the admonishment that God has given us in His Word regarding this destructive force. Proud people fool themselves into thinking they are better than others. People who think this way are easily rattled. The proud of heart seldom realize that pride is their problem, but anyone who reads human character well will quickly detect that it is.

Volunteer work is serious business and should never be taken lightly. A person with a pride problem who involves himself in volunteer work can shipwreck the good that volunteers are trying to do to help others. I saw it happen on more than one occasion during my incarceration by inmates who sabotaged a volunteer project simply because they could or because they had a beef with prison officials. That's messed up!

The way to avoid letting pride keep you from acquiring the desire to get involved in volunteer work during and after your incarceration is simply to admit that you have a problem with pride. Once you flip the script and humble yourself to the point where you can keep your pride in check, your attitude toward volunteer work will change from that of something you have no desire to do, to that of something you enjoy doing.

During my years of running the streets, and throughout my twenty-four years of incarceration, I discovered it is hard to do anything good, meaningful or worthwhile if your heart is not in it, especially if you are not right with God. There is no common ground between good and evil. You are either one or the other. *"You cannot drink the cup of the Lord and the cup of demons; you cannot have a part in the Lord's table and the table of demons"* (1 Corinthians 10:21). *"For what do righteousness and wickedness have in common? Or what fellowship can light have with darkness. What harmony is there between Christ and Belial? What does a believer have in common with an unbeliever?"* (2 Corinthians 14:14-15).

If that describes you, then I encourage you to get your heart right with God while you still have the chance. Time waits for no one. *"I tell you, now is the time of God's favor, now is the day of salvation"* (2 Corinthians 6:2b).

If you feel that getting yourself involved in a volunteer project at your facility may be the catalyst that can help you humble yourself and get rid of any pride you may have in your heart, then by all means get involved. God may just be calling you at such a time as this, for such a cause as this, in order to get your attention.

> *"If you are not sure you have a pride problem, it may be that self-centeredness has blinded you to the warning signs. Just ask someone you trust, who knows you well."*

If you are not sure you have a pride problem, it may be that self-centeredness has blinded you to the warning signs. Just ask someone you trust, who knows you well. He or she may just be able to keep you from self-destructing. *"Pride only breeds quarrels, but wisdom is found in those who take advice"* (Proverbs 13:10). *"Pride brings a person low, but the lowly in spirit gain honor"* (Proverbs 29:23). There is wisdom in these Scriptures. Meditate on them and do yourself a solid by taking heed.

Whatever you do, do not be misled into thinking you cannot get involved in volunteer work because you are incarcerated. There are many opportunities to do volunteer work in a correctional setting. Even if there are no civilian-sponsored volunteer projects at your facility, you can still create your own projects, for example, volunteering your time by helping a fellow inmate in need. Be creative. You will be surprised at the opportunities you can create on your own and get other inmates involved in.

Once you acquire the desire, you will find it easier to invest the time that is necessary to get involved in those opportunities, and/or to create your own. It is not rocket science. *"Commit your way to the LORD; trust in him and he will do this: He will make your righteousness shine like the dawn, the justice of your cause like the noonday sun"* (Psalm 37:5-6). Your part is to follow God's lead and put the gifts, talents, and skills He blessed you with to good use. *"Each one should use whatever gift he has received to serve others, faithfully administering God's grace in its various forms"* (1 Peter 4:10).

Do not sit around waiting for opportunities to come to you; *they may never come.* Instead be a wise steward of your time by looking for ways to get involved in worthwhile projects during your incarceration, be it a prison-sponsored or a community-sponsored project that you can contribute to in some way. You will be serving time productively by doing a civic duty from right where you are.

SELF-HELP GROUP

This can be one of the most effective ways to sharpen your social skills during your incarceration because you are in a productive setting with other inmates who are of the same mindset. Most correctional facilities have self-help groups of one kind or another that can be instrumental at keeping inmates focused on positive things during their incarceration. The self-help groups I got involved in at some of the facilities I was housed at did that for me during my incarceration, programs like Jaycees, CPR, and Drug Education. These were just some of the self-help programs that were offered, so I took advantage of these opportunities and benefitted a lot from them.

You too can benefit by joining a self-help group during your incarceration. Look for a group at your facility that can help you in some way, or that you might be able to contribute something to. There are groups that are connected with community organizations, businesses, and college and university programs run by professors, students, and other professionals who go into correctional facilities to hold workshops and conduct seminars that are centered on teaching inmates skills they can use during and after their incarceration. The opportunities are there; you just have to take advantage of them.

> *"I took a management course at one of the facilities I was housed at... I learned valuable management skills that I am able to use in society."*

I took a management course at one of the facilities I was housed at conducted by a McDonalds franchise owner and received a Certificate of Completion for successfully completing the course. I learned valuable management skills that I am able to use in society. On the day we received our certificates, the guy brought all the students their choice of a Big Mac, Quarter Pounder with cheese, or Filet-o-Fish, and fries and a soft drink or shake. I had a Big Mac, which I had not eaten in almost fifteen years. I no longer eat Mickey D's, but I devoured that Big Mac that day!

The benefit of having that Certificate of Completion in Restaurant Management is that I can get an entry-level job at McDonalds as an Assistant Manager, Manager, or even a Franchise Owner, if that was something I chose to pursue. The reason I chose not to pursue that opportunity upon my release is because I am committed to pursuing my God-given purpose to encourage and equip incarcerated men and women to serve their time productively, so that when they are released, they will be prepared to make the challenging transition from prison back to society and avoid reoffending. And, to my God-given vision to form a nonprofit that serves the needs of ex-offenders. That vision was birthed in my spirit while I was incarcerated after witnessing numerous men I served time with get released and return to prison on a parole violation or a new offense simply because they had no one on the outside to help them reintegrate successfully back into society. And also because they did not prepare themselves to reenter society while incarcerated by serving their time productively.

The purpose and the vision were two of the things that helped me to serve time productively while incarcerated. Although the vision is still a work in progress, it is a key element that helps me stay focused on God's purpose and plan for my life, and keeps me managing time wisely every day.

I was faithful to sow seed on good soil (Matthew 13:23), believing that when I prayed the vision I would receive it (Mark 11:24), because God is faithful to all His promises (Psalm 145:13), and He watches over His Word to perform it (Jeremiah 1:12), so that it will not return to Him empty, but accomplish all that He desires and achieve the purpose for which He sent it (Isaiah 55:11).

If you have a substance abuse problem I encourage you to join a self-help group at your facility that deals with this issue, if you have not already done so, to help kick your addiction. You might as well take advantage of this help while it is available and free of charge. Whatever your needs or interests might be, you should consider joining a self-help group at your facility that can help you or that you can be of service to. Not only will you be serving time productively during your involvement with the group, you will be sharpening your social skills and increasing your ability to make a successful transition in society when you are released.

Don't just serve your time, manage it!

THOUGHT PROVOKERS
Chapter Five: Social Time

1. In order to be a socially responsible person during your incarceration, and after you're released, it is imperative that you focus on reconciling strained relationships, building new relationships, making amends to your victim(s), establishing relationships with community-based organizations that are dedicated to helping inmates during and after their incarceration, train yourself to become an effective communicator and listener, cultivate your social skills daily so that you can be an effective people person daily, do volunteer work, join a self-help group.

   Have you/do you/will you apply any of these to your management of time? _____
   _____

2. Don't burn bridges with people you know, especially family; some of those bridges may not be repairable! If anything, you should be focused on mending broken relationships. Have you burned any bridges before or during your incarceration?

   If so, have you made any attempt to reconcile with that person(s) _____
   _____

3. When you invest time being a genuine friend to a fellow inmate, you show that person the heart of God. Have you/do you/will you invest(ed) time during your incarceration being a genuine friend to a fellow inmate? _____
   _____
   _____
   _____

4. Making amends (if possible) to the victim(s) of your case, is one of the best investments of time you can make during your incarceration. Tru or False _____

5. If you have children and are blessed to be able to communicate with them, how much time do you invest communicating with them via correspondence, by phone, or on visits, if you're able to? What values have you/do you/will you instill(ed) in them? _

   _____

   _____

   _____

6. When you invest time training yourself to be an effective communicator and listener you only partially develop, improve, and sharpen your social skills. True or False _____

7. Writing is one of the most valuable skills you can have during and after a period of incarceration. How much time have you/do you/will you invest(ed) using this valuable gift/talent/skill during your incarceration, and after you're released? _____

   _____

   _____

8. When you invest time honing your comprehension skills, you sharpen your social skills. Doing this will benefit you in your interaction with inmates and staff, and will help prepare you to reenter society by giving you a skill set (comprehension) that will enable you to better understand things that you read or hear. What steps are you taking to improve your level of comprehension? _____

   _____

9. The more time you invest learning how to be a people person while incarcerated, the better you will become at displaying it. This will benefit you during your incarceration by helping you

gain the respect of those around you and will minimize your chances of getting caught up in prison drama. When you're released, it will carry over into your relationships with family, friends, colleagues, co-workers, and whomever else God chooses to place in your life. People will gravitate towards you because of it.

Do you/have you/will you invest(ed) time learning how to become a better people person? _____

_____

_____

10. God did not put us on this earth to serve ourselves. He put us here to serve Him and others. As such, when you invest time during your incarceration connecting with a community-based organization(s) (CBO) that is dedicated to helping inmates during and after a period of incarceration, you improve your chances of making a successful transition in society and not reoffending.

Have you/do you/will you invest(ed) time while incarcerated connecting with a CBO? _____

_____

_____

What you do during your incarceration is a reflection of what you will be doing when you are released.

CONCLUSION

"Now all has been heard; here is the conclusion of the matter: fear God and keep his commandments, for this is the whole duty of man" - Ecclesiastes 12:13

As America's rate of imprisonment continues to grow, so too does the recidivism rate. There are now over two million individuals incarcerated in jails and prisons across this country. One of the consequences of this level of imprisonment is that a growing number of offenders are being released from jails and prisons and are returning to their communities.

Each year, nearly 500,000 people leave state prisons and return to communities across the United States. For some releasees who are fortunate, the process of re-entry into society will be a smooth one because they have a support foundation. Their families accept them back, employment opportunities await them, and supportive networks stand ready to keep them on the straight and narrow and to encourage them to become productive members of their communities.

For others who are less fortunate, the process of re-entry into society will be anything but smooth because they do *not* have a support foundation, their families may not be willing to accept them back, securing employment will be difficult, and individuals they might still be associating with that are involved in criminal activity will be ready to offer them that lifestyle again. Such circumstances often contribute to a releasee's return to criminal activity and subsequent recidivism. It's just a matter of when, where, and how. If you're incarcerated, and are fortunate enough to be released and are determined to make it on the outside, don't allow that to become you.

As I stated in the introduction of this book, whether you are soon to be released, still have time to serve, or are a permanent resident, you can manage time productively if you apply the principles set forth herein. In order for you to use this knowledge to your advantage and for your benefit, you must be serious about managing time. Every day has twenty-four hours filled with opportunities for you to change, grow, and be productive. Yet, it is easy to mismanage time in a correctional setting because of the stress of being incarcerated. Some inmates allow time to pass them by and never get around to doing anything productive as a result of unproductive activities they needlessly engage in. Time that is served engaging in activities that are not geared toward improving yourself is time that is squandered. If that describes you, then I ask *"How is that working out for you?"* I'm just saying! On the flip side, when you view time as a gift from God, you will be more inclined to manage it productively. Who in their right mind doesn't desire that!

Most inmates find it difficult being effective at managing time for a number of reasons, with lack of purpose topping the list. To those of you who give no thought to the importance of managing time as a result of whatever trials or tribulations you might be going through, keep in mind that whatever you have been through, are currently going through, or may yet have to go through during your incarceration, I probably went through it, and then some. There is little, if anything, in the way of trials and tribulations that I did not experience during my twenty-four years of incarceration. If I were to list just some of them, I would have to write an entire chapter based on that. But that is not the purpose of this book.

I know what it is like to have decades of time left to serve, to feel like there is no hope and no reason to try to better yourself. I know what it is like to mismanage time in a correctional setting because I mismanaged the first eight years of my forty-eight year sentence engaging in unproductive activity. If you have mismanaged any of the time you have served thus far, do not despair, you are not alone. I have been there and done that and I know how difficult it can be to flip the script and break out of that mindset. Particularly if you are involved in a lifestyle like I was (gangs, drugs, etc.) that misleads you into doing the exact opposite of everything you have read in this book.

If you are stuck on having to portray the image of being tough or hard because you feel that is the only way you will ever get respect from fellow inmates, then you are not managing time; time is managing you. As a former gang member I used to carry myself that way, thinking I was all that and believing I had to maintain a certain image of being hardcore in order to get respect. But when I snapped out of that mindless haze and realized I did not have to carry myself that way, I discovered the "real me" and began to conduct myself accordingly.

"A wicked man puts up a bold front, but an upright man gives thought to his ways" (Proverbs 21:29). To my surprise, inmates respected me more because of it.

If you desire to apply the principles set forth in this book but are currently involved in negative activities that can place you at odds with prison officials and possibly prolong your sentence, you will first have to distance yourself from that. You will need to dismiss the bravado act, if you carry yourself that way, and learn to be the person God created you to be, not the person someone else wants you to be. You will have to humble yourself and let an infallible God direct your path so that you do not allow a fallible human being to direct it for you (1 Peter 5:6; Proverbs 3:5-6).

Why be a follower of negativity when you can be a leader of positivity? Once you learn how to maximize your strengths, you will know how to minimize your weaknesses. Managing time will then become second nature to you, just as it became for me when I began to apply the principles set forth in this book.

When all is said and done, what it comes down to is this: *You alone must decide whether you are going to manage time by serving it productively or mismanage time by serving it destructively.* There is no middle ground. Try to do both and you will eventually self-destruct like many others before you have done during their incarceration. I witnessed it happen many times during my incarceration. It almost happened to me!

Most of the inmates I saw this happen to are inmates I once hung out with. They chose to stay on that destructive path long after I chose to get off of it, and the majority of them are still reaping the consequences of making that choice. Had I stayed on that path I might never have been released from prison. That was a consequence I chose to avoid and I am reaping the blessing of making that choice.

In the final analysis, to be effective at anything you do in life you need to be *disciplined and consistent.* In the area of time management, if you are serious about managing time during your incarceration so that you can serve time productively, and after your incarceration so that you can transition in society successfully, discipline and consistency are imperative. Anything short of that and you may be setting yourself up for another setback; one more serious than the one you experienced by going to prison. Moreover, every inmate with a release date needs to plan for how he or she will make the transition back to society.

If you have a release date, you should start formulating your plan a minimum of six months prior to your release; this way you will already know what you are going to do and how you are going to do it *before* you are released. Ask God for wisdom and guidance in formulating your plan. Pray over it and commit it to Him (Proverbs 16:3). Do not make the mistake of walking out of prison without a plan, and do not wait until you are released to formulate one. Failure to plan is planning to fail! *"Write down the vision; make it plain on tablets"* (Habakkuk 2:2).

Get involved in pre-release classes, even if they are not mandatory at your facility. These classes can help prepare you for things you will have to deal with in society, such as resume writing, cover letters, interviewing skills, job hunting, housing, food, shelter, just to name a few. These classes should actually be called "post-release" classes, since these are all post-release issues you will be dealing with. Either way, if they offer these classes at your facility I encourage you to enroll in them. They could mean the difference between making a successful re-entry in society and being the next recidivism statistic.

Certainly there are many other books written by former inmates that are packed with useful information on a variety of topics, including how to serve time productively and how to make a successful transition back to society. I am certain each one of those books is serving a specific purpose. I believe, however, the book you are holding is in a league of its own, simply because I have yet to read a book written by a former inmate that covers the topic of time management in a correctional setting from a *Christian* perspective. This is a God project. What you have in your hands is a powerful, life-changing piece of literature that you can benefit from. All you have to do now is apply what you have learned.

Everything you have read in this book can be applied by anyone who is incarcerated, whether male or female, adult or juvenile. It does not matter what your religious preference might be, because God is no respecter of persons. My use of Scripture throughout the text comes from my faith in Christ. *"Choose you whom you will serve this day. As for me and my household we shall serve the LORD"* (Joshua 24:15).

It does not matter whether you are soon to be released, still have time to serve, or are a permanent resident. The only thing that matters is that you apply what you have learned from this book so that you can benefit from it and be successful at managing time both during and after your incarceration. Do this and you will avoid contributing to the recidivism rate. This is a win-win for you and for all of society. Run with it. I am.

Shalom!

> "...The LORD bless you and keep you; the LORD make his face shine upon you and be gracious to you; the LORD turn his face toward you and give you peace" - Numbers 6:24-25

REMINDERS FOR TIME MANAGEMENT

SPIRIT TIME:
Have faith in God and give Him first place in your life / Pray regularly on your own and with fellow believers / Establish a regular time of personal Bible study / Attend group Bible study / Get involved in Chapel activities.

SOUL TIME:
Do not allow your mind to become idle; use it wisely / Educate yourself academically or vocationally / Maintain a work detail / Become computer literate / Cultivate your gifts, talents, and skills and use them for God's glory, not yours.

PHYSICAL TIME:
Exercise regularly / Eat properly / Drink enough water / Get enough sleep each day; take naps / Stay away from body killers (cigarettes, drugs, alcohol).

MONEY TIME:
Learn everything you can about managing money / Tithe / Give to those in need / Save as much as you can so that you'll have something to fall back on when you are released / Establish a budget and stick to it / Invest wisely / Be disciplined in the way you spend money.

SOCIAL TIME:

Reconcile strained relationships / Build new relationships / Make amends to your victim(s) / Invest time in your children / Train yourself to become an effective communicator, listener, and speaker / Develop people skills / Connect with community-based organizations / Become a volunteer / Join a self-help group.

SUGGESTED READINGS

SPIRIT TIME:

- The Laws of Study and Meditation, by Hiram Gomez
- Blueprint of A God Man, by Ellis C. McCarthy
- 21 Irrefutable Laws of Leadership, by John Maxwell
- A Better Way to Pray / You've Already Got It / God Wants You Well by Andrew Wommack
- Transform Your Thinking / The Kingdom of God In You / Power of the Tithe by Bill Winston
- Prayer Confessions to Dominate In the New Millennium by Veronica Winston
- Prayer—Your Foundation for Success / Prosperity: The Choice Is Yours / From Faith to Faith (with Gloria Copeland) by Kenneth Copeland
- Love—The Secret to Your Success, by Gloria Copeland
- Understanding the Power and Purpose of Prayer / The Principles and Power of Vision / The Spirit of Leadership, by Dr. Myles Munroe
- Hope Again, by Charles Swindoll
- Faith Can Change Your World, by Lester Sumrall
- The Purpose Driven Life, by Rick Warren

- How to Listen to God, by Charles Stanley
- Spiritual Warfare, by Derek Prince
- Walking In Your Destiny, by Juanita Bynum
- The Prayer That Changes Everything, by Stormie Omartian
- A Wife's Prayer, by Pamela Hines
- Behold, Thy Handmaid / Broken Vessels / From Pain To Purpose / Out of the Septic Tank / Pictures From Heaven, by Chris McQuay
- Reboot Your Marriage, by Wes and Neesha Stringfellow
- Rebirth and Rejoice / How To Be Happy and Successfully Single, by Tina Swain
- Fresh Air, by Chris Hodges

Soul Time:
- The Mind of Christ, by T.W. Hunt
- Soul Detox, by Craig Groeschel
- The Warrior's Soul, by William G. Boykin and Stu Webber
- Soul Keeping: Caring For The Most Important Part of You, by John Ortberg
- Today God Is First, by Os Hillman

Body Time:
- Body by God / Extreme Makeover God's Way / Winning My Race, by Dr. Ben Lerner
- Transforming You, by Dr. Rhonda Mayes
- The Body Sculpting Bible for Men, by James Villepigue and H.A. Rivera
- Encyclopedia of Bodybuilding, by Arnold Schwarzenegger
- God Wants You Well, by Andrew Wommack

- Fat Free Forever, by Bobby Ray
- The Maker's Diet, by Jordan Rubin
- Take Control of Your Health, by Dr. Joseph Mercola
- The Seven Pillars of Health / Toxic Relief , by Dr. Don Colbert
- 10 Essentials of Highly Healthy People, by Walt Larimore
- Body for Life, by Bill Phillips
- MEN'S HEALTH (magazine)
- MUSCLE & FITNESS (magazine; men and women)
- SHAPE (women's magazine)

MONEY TIME:

- God's Plan for Prosperity, by Mark Gorman
- Think Like a Billionaire, Become a Billionaire, by Scot Anderson
- Your Money Map / Your Money Counts, by Howard Dayton
- Rich Dad, Poor Dad / Cash Flow Quadrant / Guide to Investing, by Robert Kiyosaki
- Reallionaire, by Farrah Gray
- The One Minute Millionaire, by Mark Victor Hansen and Robert G. Allen
- FORBES (magazine)
- ENTREPRENEUR (magazine)
- FAST COMPANY (magazine)
- INC (magazine)
- BLACK ENTERPRISE (magazine)
- HISPANIC (magazine)

SOCIAL TIME:

- Undoing Time: American Prisoners In Their Own Words (Paperback, Kindle) by Jeff Evans
- Changed Imagination, Changed Obedience, by Natalie K. Houghty-Haddon
- Basics For Communicating by Ed Shewan and Garry J. Moes
- Listening Effectively: Achieving High Standards in Communications, Edition 1, by John A. Kline
- Communicating Effectively, Edition 1, by Lani Arredondo and Roger A. Formisano
- Everyone Communicates, Few Connect, by John C. Maxwell
- How To Write Anything: A Guide and Reference With Readings, Edition 2, by John J. Ruszkiewicz
- Volunteering: A How-To Guide, by Audrey Borus

SUGGESTED VIEWING CHANNELS

- TBN
- CBN
- MCTV
- JCTV
- CNN
- FOX BUSINESS NETWORK
- PBS
- HISTORY CHANNEL
- DISCOVERY CHANNEL
- EXERCISE TV

TIME THIEVES

- Any activity you might be spending too much time engaging in that does not contribute to your personal growth and development.

- Inmates who are not serving time productively.

- Unrealistic goals.

TIME TOOLS

- Bible with a Concordance and Dictionary - Read, study, and meditate on it daily. Therein lies your blessing.

- Daily Planner - Never start your day until you finish it on paper. Write it out. And then do your best to work it out.

- Your skills, talents, and gifts; Use them daily.

- Community Based Organizations - Contact them, and build relationships that will help you stay positive when you're released.

**24-hour information hotline for ex-offenders:
1-800-DA-BRIDGE**

The Author
LALO GOMEZ

Lalo Gomez was born in Puerto Rico and moved to Chicago with his family at the age of one.

He joined a gang at age twelve and by age fifteen was heavily-involved in a destructive lifestyle of gang banging, drug trafficking, and boosting cars for a multi-million dollar auto theft ring. For the next three years, gang life is all he lived and breathed. At age eighteen, he had a son and decided to change course, but by then it was too late, his past had already caught up to him. Less than two years later, Lalo was arrested and eventually convicted of his role in several gang-related crimes.

The consequences of Lalo's destructive lifestyle resulted in a prison term of 48-years (the prosecutors asked for life without parole) of which he served twenty-four years. During that time he experienced the harsh and oftentimes violent world of prison life up close and personal. After grossly mismanaging the first eight years of his prison term, Lalo chose to put gang life behind him. Not one to commit to anything half-heartedly, he set out to manage time and serve the remainder of his sentence as productively as one can in the correctional setting. By the grace of God, he was able to achieve that goal. This book serves as evidence that turning a negative into a positive is achievable for those who commit themselves to change, whether incarcerated or not.

Lalo was released from prison in 2008 and has since made a successful transition in society by following the principles he writes about in this book. Because of this, he has proved that ex-offenders *can* make a successful transition in society and help to reduce the recidivism rate *if* they prepare themselves during their incarceration by serving (managing) their time productively. His God-given purpose in life is to encourage and equip incarcerated men and women to serve their time productively so that when they are released, they will be prepared to make their reentry in society, avoid reoffending, and be able to fulfill their God-given purpose in life.

Lalo's interests include writing, business and sports, and he is an active member of his local church. Lalo has an Associate's Degree in General Education from Illinois Central College and is Managing Partner and Co-Founder of PFL Solutions, a business that provides publishing and information technology services.

Please contact the author at:
MANAGING TIME
388 Bullsboro Drive #338
Newnan, GA 30263

email: managingtime247@gmail.com